Prayers
for
Hope and
Healing

SARAH FORGRAVE

HARVEST HOUSE PUBLISHERS
EUGENE, OREGON

PRAYERS FOR HOPE AND HEALING

Copyright © 2017 by Sarah Forgrave
Published by Harvest House Publishers
Eugene, Oregon 97402
www.harvesthousepublishers.com

ISBN 978-0-7369-7151-5 (Hardcover)
ISBN 978-0-7369-7152-2 (eBook)

Printed in China

17 18 19 20 21 22 23 24 25 / RDS-JC / 10 9 8 7 6 5 4 3 2 1

For the Ultimate Physician—
Healer, Sustainer, and Giver of Hope

Contents

Hope in the Storm

I'll never forget the morning my life changed forever. My baby boy had decided to make an early arrival into the world, and as I scrambled to contact my workplace and organize the other pieces of my life, one thought pulsed through my mind.

Life will never be the same again.

I had no idea how true those words would be, but in a far different way than I could have imagined.

The birth of any firstborn throws a parent's life into a whirlwind, but my son's delivery left me with internal injuries my doctor couldn't repair. My symptoms were deeply personal, humiliating, and so rare that I couldn't find any friends who had heard of them, let alone experienced them.

As I transitioned home after the delivery, my maternity leave stretched into long-term disability. I spent a year and a half in doctors' offices, endured multiple colorectal surgeries, and watched others care for my son because my procedures prevented me from lifting more than eight pounds. As a healthy, growing baby, my son had quickly surpassed that mark, so my husband took him to daycare on weekdays while I sat at home alone, dealing with the ugly realities of my condition and questioning if life was worth living.

I wasn't a complete stranger to the medical world—my sister had survived cancer and a bone marrow transplant when we were kids—but going through my own health crisis awakened me to the challenges, humiliation, and pain that come with a chronic condition.

By God's grace, I made it through that time fully healed, but my journey hasn't remained easy since then. I've had a Cesarean birth with complications and two partial hysterectomies, all while supporting my sister through a heart transplant and housing her in the month afterward.

If there's one thing I've learned, it's that nothing in life is guaranteed. Tomorrow may bring sickness, or it may bring healing. It may knock you down yet again, or it may reveal a sliver of hope. As I've faced illness and pain, I've doubted God's faithfulness, yelled at Him for not healing me, and felt utterly alone.

But through it all—even in the isolation, fear, and despair—I've sensed His presence. I've felt it in passages of Scripture discovered in doctors' waiting rooms, in faint whispers of hope heard in the dark of night, in the hands and feet of friends offering their help.

Even when God feels far away, His love is real.

Whether you're facing illness, injury, or disability right now, I'm guessing you've picked up this book with the goal of finding solace and hope. Maybe your situation has left you so scarred that this is your last resort to numb the pain. As someone who's been there, I pray these pages will soothe your fears and minister to your spirit.

Using my own experiences and those of my sister, I've written *Prayers for Hope and Healing* as a manual for navigating emotions you may face. You're welcome to read it from front to back, or it can be used as a menu of sorts. When you face a particular situation, you can let the Contents page guide you to what you need.

As you read, remember this truth: *You are not alone.* God's love for you is everlasting, and He will see you through.

I pray this book blesses you in these challenging days.

Sarah

1

When There's No End in Sight

For those facing a long-term health
situation that feels endless.

*A large crowd followed and pressed around him. And
a woman was there who had been subject to bleeding
for twelve years. She had suffered a great deal under
the care of many doctors and had spent all she had, yet
instead of getting better she grew worse. When she heard
about Jesus, she came up behind him in the crowd and
touched his cloak, because she thought, "If I just touch
his clothes, I will be healed"… At once Jesus realized
that power had gone out from him. He turned around
and asked, "Who touched my clothes?"*

MARK 5:24-28,30

—ഝ—

No end in sight. Does that describe how you feel
right now? Whether you've been dealing with

your condition for one week or many years, you may feel like the road you're on will never end.

My friend, let this passage in the Bible lift your gaze beyond your current situation to a God who not only sees your pain, but *feels* it. This woman was out of money and out of hope. She'd visited countless doctors with no cure to show for it. Scripture doesn't specify how she approached Jesus—just that she came up behind Him—but I've often imagined her on her knees, squeezing between legs and feet, stretching until her arm ached to touch the edge of Jesus's cloak.

Immediately her touch was felt.

Immediately.

No matter how long the journey ahead of you, Jesus invites you to drop to your knees and reach out for Him. You might not receive physical healing like this woman did, but He'll provide what you need for today. He sees you and loves you.

Are you ready to come to Him?

Dear Lord,

I'll be honest. Stories in the Bible that tell of Your immediate healing frustrate me sometimes. Why would You choose to heal some who are sick, while others of us are left to deal with our conditions indefinitely? There are moments when I feel trapped in the middle of a dark tunnel. I try to take steps forward—to keep hope alive—but it seems as though I'll never see light again.

Even as my strength dwindles, will You renew my hope? Will You show me a ray of light to keep me going? I acknowledge that You have the power to heal, and I ask You to bring life to my body if it's in Your will. But if it's Your will to keep me on this road a while longer, help me to accept Your plan with grace and trust.

If there's something You want to develop within me, give me vision to see my weak spots and the humility to accept that I can't change on my own. Help me to come to You for all I need. As I wake up each day with no new healing, and frustration and despair wash over me yet again, remind me of Your faithfulness. Give me what I need to make it through each moment. I commit to seeking truth in Your Word and in prayer so I can be armed with all I need for this battle.

Thank You for not only seeing my condition but for feeling my pain. I reach out to You now for my comfort and strength.

In Jesus's name, amen.

2

When You Can't Sleep

For those who need rest but find
themselves lying awake.

*In peace I will lie down and sleep, for you alone, L*ORD*,
make me dwell in safety.*

PSALM 4:8

—⁓—

Almost nothing frustrates more than tossing and turning when you should be sleeping instead. Maybe
you're lying awake because of strange hospital noises or
beeping monitors. Maybe the effects of medication have
made you wired, spiking your awareness of every sight,
sound, and sensation in your body. Maybe worries are
buzzing through your mind, launching a full-on attack
against your ability to relax.

Whatever the cause, release your frustrations to the
One who offers a safe landing pad. Imagine the thoughts

and distractions floating from your shoulders and resting on Almighty God, who never slumbers nor sleeps. He can handle each one.

Even in this environment where sleep eludes you and your troubles feel larger than life, remember He is always watching over you. He's here with you now, inviting you to come to Him. As you talk with Him, He'll cover you with His peace and bring the rest you need.

Will you come to Him now?

—◦◦◦—

Dear Lord,

My body is so tired, but here I am, wide awake and talking to You. I wish I could change the circumstances keeping me awake—could take away the distractions and worries heightening my awareness—but I know it's not always possible.

Even as my frustration mounts, I thank You for this chance to spend extra time with You. My body may struggle to rest, but I know You offer a safe place of peace. Will You fill me with that peace now?

If I need to take any steps to remove distractions in my room, show me what those steps should be. If I need to release any worries to You, I offer them to You with open hands. I recognize that worrying doesn't fix my problems; it only steals my strength for tomorrow. I need all the strength I can get, so I pass these concerns into Your hands and commit to resting in You.

Whether I'm able to sleep or not, I pray You would fill my mind and heart with "soul rest"—the kind that comes from knowing You are here. Not only are You watching over me, You're communing with me, inviting me into the safety of Your presence. As I allow the things of this world to slip from my awareness, I rest in You. I proclaim You the Lord of peace and the Lord of my life.

In Jesus's name, amen.

3

When You Don't Understand God's Plan

For those who struggle to see the bigger picture of God's plan in their suffering.

[Jesus] withdrew about a stone's throw beyond them, knelt down and prayed, "Father, if you are willing, take this cup from me; yet not my will, but yours be done."

LUKE 22:41-42

Though you have made me see troubles, many and bitter, you will restore my life again; from the depths of the earth you will again bring me up. You will increase my honor and comfort me once more.

PSALM 71:20-21

—⁓—

I t's not fair." Have you said those words to God? Maybe not out loud, but in your mind? The reality is, those words are true. Life is hard and unfair, and sometimes we find ourselves wondering if God still loves us.

If this describes you, I pray you'll find comfort in the nail-scarred hands of Jesus. If anyone was forced into an unfair situation, it was the Son of God, who came to earth to take on the pain of the whole world. In the final hours before His death, He cried out in prayer, asking for a way out. And yet He still chose to say, "Not my will, but yours be done."

Your suffering may not make sense. It may seem unbearable and downright cruel at times. But what if you believed there could be joy after this pain? What if you believed that just as God raised Jesus from the dead, He can bring life to your situation too? He may restore you in a different way and time frame than you would choose, but keep holding on. There is hope ahead.

Will you seek it in Him?

—⟋⟋⟋—

Dear Lord,

I feel the brunt of my condition every day, and I won't lie. It's pushed me to a place of asking hard questions. I don't understand why You would allow this kind of pain in my life. I see the way it impacts not only me, but also my loved ones, and I can't grasp how a kind, loving God could allow such suffering.

Even as I struggle with my doubts, I'm thankful for the reminder that Your Son faced unbearable pain too, and His suffering wasn't without purpose. His example inspires me to open myself up to Your will, even when it's hard. Thank You that Your plans are always for ultimate good—that You see the bigger picture and promise to comfort those who are broken and hurting.

That's me right now—broken and hurting. All I see in front of me is more suffering and pain. As I try to grasp Your purpose in all of this, please shift my eyes from my circumstances and keep them focused on You. When I can't see down the road to understand the "why," fill me with more faith so I can see You working here and now.

Remind me often of the power of prayer. I commit to bringing my questions and doubts to You, no matter how ugly or "unspiritual" they seem. I know You welcome me just as I am, and I choose to come to You first as my source of purpose and hope.

In Jesus's name, amen.

4

When You Feel Abandoned by Your Friends

For those who have dropped off their
friends' priority lists.

*At my first defense, no one came to my support, but
everyone deserted me. May it not be held against them.
But the Lord stood at my side and gave me strength.*

2 TIMOTHY 4:16-17

———

As if life weren't difficult enough, physical challenges
can add distance between you and your friends.
Not just the distance defined by miles and streets, but
the distance felt through quiet phones and lonely souls.

Whether your condition has landed you in the hospital or at home, friends may drop you from their priority lists for a number of reasons. Maybe their schedule is
overloaded, and they don't know how to add one more

thing. Maybe they're reeling from your situation, and their method of coping is to keep their distance. Maybe they don't know what to say, so they feel safer not saying anything.

No matter the reason, I pray you'll find comfort in the words of Paul. Even a great hero of the faith—one who lived in step with God's Spirit—felt forgotten and alone at times. While people let him down, deserting him to handle his trials alone, he drew strength from the presence of God.

That same God offers His presence to you right now. You may be disappointed or hurt by your friends' abandonment, but God offers a safe place of belonging. He isn't too busy to stand by your side.

Will you draw your strength from Him?

—ᴧᴧᴧ—

Dear Lord,

I feel so alone right now. Not only am I struggling with my physical condition, but the loss of my friends has poured salt on the wound. Whether they've meant to hurt me or not, their lack of contact makes me feel as though I'm too much of a burden for them to be bothered.

I recognize that my self-confidence is already low. As I deal with my physical challenges and struggle to find glimpses of my old self, I'm more vulnerable to being hurt by others. As hard as my friends' abandonment is, I don't want it to define who I am. Will You help me find my value and self-worth in You?

Thank You for the reminder that even heroes of the faith felt deserted at times, and yet Your presence never wavered. Lord, I believe You are the same yesterday, today, and forever, so I can say with confidence that You are here with me now. When the loneliness crowds in and my phone remains silent, may Your presence bring me comfort.

Help me bring my friends to You in prayer. I know they're dealing with their own struggles. I want to use this time to soften my heart, not let it harden with hurt and bitterness. Show me ways I can reach out to them and offer Your forgiveness and love. Just as I want others to show me grace in my condition, I want to extend that same grace to them.

Thank You that my value and worth are found in You alone, and the choices of others can never change that fact. Please keep me out of the trap of self-pity, and ground me in Your love. I place my identity in Your hands.

In Jesus's name, amen.

5

When You Feel Angry

For those who are angry at their
situation and ultimately at God
for allowing their pain.

*O Lord, how long will you forget me? Forever?
How long will you look the other way? How long
must I struggle with anguish in my soul, with sorrow
in my heart every day? How long will my enemy
have the upper hand? Turn and answer me, O LORD
my God! Restore the sparkle to my eyes, or I will die.
Don't let my enemies gloat, saying, "We have
defeated him!" Don't let them rejoice at my downfall.
But I trust in your unfailing love. I will rejoice
because you have rescued me.*

PSALM 13:1-5 NLT

Anger can sweep in at any moment, consuming you
until your jaw clenches and your prayers toss bitter

words at God. "How much longer will You make me suffer?" "Why don't You just *do* something already?"

This kind of anger pulses through the words in Psalm 13. Anger, frustration, impatience—all directed at the God of the universe. Maybe you can relate to the psalmist. Maybe your condition has pushed you to the point of no longer accepting, but all-out blaming. My friend, rest assured you are not alone.

Just as God invited the psalmist to come to Him unfiltered—to lay his frustrations and anger at Jesus's feet—He invites you to do the same. He can handle your anger. He can handle the questions and blame and fear. As you release them to Him, He will cover you with His unfailing love, turning your honest confession into a song of praise.

Will you allow Him to work in your heart right now?

—⁓—

Dear Lord,

I relate to the psalmist's words all too well. I'm not just frustrated; I'm downright angry. I don't understand why You would let me suffer like this, why You wouldn't change my circumstances or heal me sooner. While everything within me wants to scream, "This isn't fair," I hesitate to say those words because they sound so childish and ungrateful.

Thank You for the reminder that You can handle my anger. You welcome the hard questions and offer a listening ear when I don't understand. I recognize that much of my anger stems from fear—fear of the unknown, fear of the pain I'll have to endure, and fear that I'll never experience healing this side of heaven.

As I bring my anger and fears to You, I thank You for providing a safe place, but I also ask that You won't let me dwell in this shell of anger forever. I recognize that it will only harden my spirit and choke my trust.

Thank You for the example of the psalmist trusting in Your unfailing love, even in the midst of his questions. I'll admit that trust doesn't come naturally to me, but I want it in my life. Would You soften the edges of my anger so I can see the ways You're working? Bring to mind the times You've been faithful in the past. Show me how I can move into a place of peace and gratitude. I offer my anger to You and ask You to reshape me.

In Jesus's name, amen.

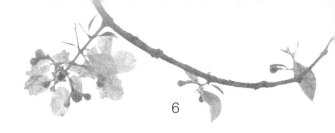

6

When You Feel Caught in a Vicious Cycle

For those who are tired of facing the
same challenges over and over.

*Have I not commanded you? Be strong and courageous.
Do not be afraid; do not be discouraged, for the LORD
your God will be with you wherever you go.*

JOSHUA 1:9

———〜———

Whether it's sitting in another medical office, feeling the sting of another needle poke, or repeating your health history for the umpteenth time, health challenges seem to bring a multitude of déjà vu moments. Sometimes they string together until you feel as though you'll never get out.

If you find yourself caught in an endless cycle, facing the same scenarios or questions time and time again, I pray you'll find rest in God's presence. He walks with you in all circumstances, at all times. He doesn't abandon you just because you're in the same place you were last week. He's been with you through it all and will continue to walk by your side.

As you grow weary of your situation—or dread feeling the same pain all over again—draw near to Him as your source of peace. Your circumstances might remain the same, but He will equip you to walk through each moment with courage and strength.

Will you allow Him to do that now?

———

Dear Lord,

Sometimes my life feels like a carnival ride, spinning in circles, and I'm strapped in with no way to escape. The same situations whirl past me—another doctor visit, another day of pain, another list of questions that have to be answered—and I'm powerless to change my course.

In the midst of this cycle, I confess that I find myself losing hope. Will I ever be delivered from these scenarios that repeat themselves over and over? Will I ever be healed? Will I ever have the chance to move on with my life? I don't know the answers to those questions, but I trust that You do.

Thank You for the reminder that You walk by my side through all of these moments, even the ones that repeat. Not only do You walk by my side, but You offer me strength and courage to get through each day.

If there are opportunities to show Your love to those I meet, I pray You will open my eyes to see them. If You're crossing my path with someone on a regular basis, give me the courage to extend Your love and to share the ways You're working in my life. Even in my weariness of this process, I don't want to miss the chance to be a light for You.

Whether it's the tenth or hundredth time I face the same scenario, I lean into Your strength. I trust that You will provide what I need. I commit to seeking You for the patience and grace to make it through.

In Jesus's name, amen.

7

When You Feel Far from God

For those who feel that God
has abandoned them
and doesn't care.

Where can I go from your Spirit?
Where can I flee from your presence?
If I go up to the heavens, you are there;
if I make my bed in the depths, you are there.
If I rise on the wings of the dawn,
if I settle on the far side of the sea,
even there your hand will guide me,
your right hand will hold me fast.

PSALM 139:7-10

Pain and trials may draw you closer to God, but other times they leave you feeling more alone than ever.

You might find yourself asking, "Where is God in all of this? Does He see me? Does He even care?"

My friend, I promise He has not abandoned you. You may barely see a glimpse of His presence. You may feel the deep thirst in your soul from losing contact with Him, but He can be found even in the hidden shadows of life.

The psalmist says God is found in the heavens and in the depths, in every corner of the earth, from those that are seen to those that are unseen. Wherever you are right now, reading these words, He is here with you.

He offers His guiding hand—a steadying presence to walk you through these moments that feel anything but stable.

Will you take hold of Him now?

—⁓—

Dear Lord,

My condition has added many challenges to my life, but the most difficult is the feeling that You've left me to deal with this on my own. Are You still there? Sometimes I wonder and doubt. The emptiness consumes me at times, filling me with the fear that I'll never get through this. It's all I can do to put one foot in front of the other.

As I struggle to find glimpses of You, I'm grateful for the reminder that You're not limited by time and space. Your presence reaches every corner of the globe—even this dark one where I find myself. Please remind me of this truth often. In my moments of questioning and despair, please show me a glimpse of Your presence. I want to know beyond a shadow of a doubt that You are real and with me, so I commit to looking for You even now.

Give me courage to hold on to the steady hand You offer. As I fall into the trap of believing I'm alone, I tend to also believe I have to travel this road by my own strength. The truth is that my strength is spent. I can't do this on my own anymore, so I turn to You for guidance and help.

As I seek You, lead me to passages of Scripture that remind me of Your presence. I want to come to Your Word first when I doubt, so the messages of the world can't take root in my mind.

Thank You for being here with me now. I commit to finding my comfort in You alone.

In Jesus's name, amen.

8

When You Feel Helpless

For those who are physically limited and can't do things for themselves.

Whom have I in heaven but you? And earth has nothing I desire besides you. My flesh and my heart may fail, but God is the strength of my heart and my portion forever.

PSALM 73:25-26

—⁓—

Whether you're recovering from surgery, dealing with an injury, or facing a long-term disability, your physical restrictions can push you past the point of frustration. Maybe you're unable to sit up without help. Maybe you can't walk to the restroom on your own, or you can't bring a forkful of food to your mouth without spilling.

Whatever the task, relying on others for basic needs can test your patience and strain the relationships with those helping you. Is it possible to be at peace when you feel so helpless?

Even if your limitations don't change, let this Scripture in Psalms remind you that God will provide all you need. This world will fail you. Your body will wear down. Other people won't always be there when you need them. But God never fails.

His strength is enough. *He* is enough.

Your physical challenges may not disappear, but He longs to fill you with vision to see your circumstances with new eyes. Peace and trust are yours if you look to Him.

Will you do that now?

—∿—

Dear Lord,

These physical limitations are wearing me out. Being forced to rely on others for basic tasks is humiliating and frustrating. I wish I could snap my fingers and make everything go back to normal again. I recognize that my physical condition may not change immediately—or maybe not even this side of heaven—but I want to see beyond the problems of today.

Will You show me how to do that? Teach me how to keep my focus on You. Like the psalmist, I want You to be my portion. I know very well that the world will let me down. My body may not recover the way I hope. My caregivers may not come to my aid when I need them. But I don't want my well-being to be based on the things of this world.

When helplessness threatens to consume me, draw me back to Your Word. Fill me with a thirst for Your truth so the only thing that will bring satisfaction is time with You. As I spend extra minutes with those who are charged with my care, show me opportunities to share Your love. My caregivers may be surrounded by patients who lash out in anger, and I don't want to do the same. I want others to see something different in me—a difference that comes from living in Your presence.

Even though it seems impossible right now, I pray You will expand my lens to see these limitations as a blessing. Whether they give me more time with You or allow me to spread Your love to others who may otherwise never see it, I want to accept my condition with grace and peace.

I trust in Your plan even when it's inconvenient for me. I commit to leaning on You during this time.

In Jesus's name, amen.

9

When You Feel Like an Inconvenience

For those who feel like a burden
to their loved ones.

You have taken account of my wanderings;
put my tears in Your bottle.
Are they not recorded in Your book?

PSALM 56:8 AMP

My God is my rock,
in whom I find protection.
He is my shield,
the power that saves me,
and my place of safety.

2 SAMUEL 22:3 NLT

———

Y ou can see it in their eyes, in the weary drag of their
feet. Your condition is taxing those you love, and

you're powerless to do anything about it. They may not say anything for fear of hurting your feelings, but you know the truth. While your condition erodes your own strength and trust, it also reaches those who watch you struggle.

Your loved ones may be directly involved in your care or they may not, but their burden can be felt. It might reveal itself through quiet tears or harsh words of impatience. It might be heard in a deep sigh or in a rushed message on the way to another commitment. No matter how it manifests itself, you're left feeling like an inconvenience—a burden.

Dear friend, let me reassure you that no matter how your situation impacts your loved ones, you are *not* a burden to God. He notices every hurt, every tear. Not only does He notice them, He collects them as a remembrance.

You may feel on edge when loved ones come to visit, knowing you're causing them pain, but you can find a safe place in the Rock of Ages. He is a strong shield who offers protection from the burden of guilt and pain.

Will you seek shelter in Him now?

Dear Lord,

I hate watching my loved ones suffer as a result of my condition. Even though I'm dealing with it firsthand, I know it's impacting them in tangible ways, especially those involved in my care. I can't help but feel bad for causing their pain. I know I'm not intentionally burdening them, but guilt is creeping in anyway.

While I would love to change this situation and remove the burden from all of us, I know that's not possible. I'm thankful that in the midst of these difficulties, You see every teardrop and hear each word of sorrow and pain. Whether the teardrops and words are mine or a loved one's, I'm humbled that You watch over us with tender care.

When I'm tempted to fall into the trap of guilt, will You remind me of Your love? You not only watch over me, providing what I need in this moment, but You also watch over my loved ones. I may not be able to remove their burden, but You can provide what they need. Help me to release them to Your care.

At the same time, I ask for open eyes to see ways I might reduce their burden. I'm thankful for the sacrifices they've made for me. If I've placed unnecessary demands on their time and energy, reveal it to me so I can make it right. Even if I can't remove the burden on their bodies or their calendars, show me ways I can ease the burden on their souls, whether through encouragement or gratitude.

Above all, I want to keep my eyes on You. When a loved one's burden expresses itself in stinging words or careless actions, remind me that You are a safe place of shelter. You are never burdened by my pain, and You welcome me into the shadow of Your wings.

I choose to rest there now.

In Jesus's name, amen.

10

When You Feel Mistreated

For those who are treated thoughtlessly
or disrespectfully by medical staff.

*Two blind men were sitting by the roadside, and
when they heard that Jesus was going by, they shouted,
"Lord, Son of David, have mercy on us!" The crowd
rebuked them and told them to be quiet, but they
shouted all the louder, "Lord, Son of David, have
mercy on us!" Jesus stopped and called them. "What
do you want me to do for you?" he asked. "Lord," they
answered, "we want our sight." Jesus had compassion
on them and touched their eyes. Immediately they
received their sight and followed him.*

MATTHEW 20:30-34

Even though most medical staff are kind and loving, others can leave you bruised and broken inside.
Their actions may be as blatant as a careless needle poke

or a reprimand for requesting help, or as subtle as an eye roll or a quiet sigh.

If you face mistreatment of any kind, let this story of Jesus remind you that your heavenly Father isn't limited by human bias or emotion. These two blind men had lived a lifetime of physical challenge, left to sit on a dusty roadside begging for help. They'd likely gotten used to the heat of the sun, the sting of dirt hitting their skin as people's sandals barely missed them. While the whole world told them to be quiet—to stop bothering important people—Jesus saw their faith and healed them.

What a beautiful promise this passage gives. As you fight your illness, you may feel uncared for when doctors or nurses focus more on their agenda than your well-being. In these moments, remember that God always sees. He mourns the hurtful attitudes and responses of those charged with your care. He draws you close and whispers, "I love you. Come rest here with Me."

Will you accept the invitation?

—⁓—

Dear Lord,

As I rely on others for my care, I'm reminded that doctors, nurses, and other caregivers are human just like me. Many of them have been wonderful so far, but the few who have been rude or impatient have left me broken. At a time when I already feel helpless, their lack of consideration makes me feel as though I'm a number to be pushed through the system. As I struggle with the aftermath of their treatment, I pray You will remind me of Your everlasting love.

Thank You for seeing me and caring about me where I am right now. You look beyond my medical chart, my never-ending needs, and my ragged appearance to see the person beneath. When my caregivers let me down, I pray Your arms would wrap around me, reminding me I'm Your child.

Help me release my doctors and nurses from a position only You can hold. I know they're prone to mistakes, just as I am. I put my faith and trust in You as the One who will never fail me. Release my hurt and anger over situations that feel unjust, and help me to place the offenders in Your hands. I want to live in the freedom of forgiveness, rather than letting frustration and bitterness chew away at my spirit.

If I need to stand up for myself, give me courage to do so with grace and dignity. Fill me with Your love so I can shine Your light to those who need it most. I turn to You alone for my comfort and help.

In Jesus's name, amen.

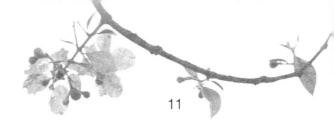

When You Feel Misunderstood

For those who feel
that no one understands
their struggles.

*All my longings lie open before you, Lord; my sighing
is not hidden from you. My heart pounds, my
strength fails me; even the light has gone from my
eyes. My friends and companions avoid me because
of my wounds; my neighbors stay far away...LORD,
I wait for you; you will answer, Lord my God.*

PSALM 38:9-11,15

Your friends and family don't mean to do it, but their responses leave you feeling alone. You can see in their eyes that they don't understand your struggle. They might try, but how can they grasp the depth of pain and fear you feel?

"I'll pray for you" and "I'm sorry" pass through their

lips, but the words are spoken hastily while the person rushes off to something else. You're crossed off their to-do list—a neat, tidy line of completion in the midst of their busy lives. Does anyone have the time and patience to listen and understand?

When loved ones fail to relate to your struggles, remember that you are understood and loved by God. He is never too busy or impatient to listen to your cries. You are never a check mark on a prayer list or calendar to Him.

He sees the depth of your pain. He feels the fear you're battling every day. He has experienced every emotion known to man through His Son Jesus, so nothing is off limits.

Even if no one understands your struggle here on earth, God invites you to come to Him. He remains faithful and present.

Will you draw comfort from Him now?

—–␣␣—

Dear Lord,

I know they have good intentions, but friends and family don't seem to have the time or interest to understand my struggle, and I'll admit it hurts. I recognize that my situation is hard. It's not pretty, and it doesn't fit in a neat and tidy box. But I would love for someone to sit down and take the time to understand—to listen and care.

Even if no one does, I'm grateful *You* listen and care. Thank You that You sent Your Son to this earth to face isolation and pain. Because of His sacrifice, I don't have to feel alone in my challenges. What a compassionate God You are—offering such an amazing gift. I'm humbled and comforted by Your love for me.

When I struggle to feel understood, please bring me back to this place. Fill me with awareness of Your presence drawing near. I ask for grace and forgiveness to flood my heart so that I can extend it to those who unknowingly hurt my feelings. I know they're doing the best they can, and many times they're facing their own fears and insecurities of how to respond to my situation. Soften me to love them as You do—without judgment or condemnation.

Most of all, keep me grounded in You. As I struggle with insecurity and loneliness, I want to seek You for everything I need. I rest in Your loving care and look to You for my comfort.

In Jesus's name, amen.

12

When You Feel Restless

For those whose bodies are itching to move
but are restricted by doctors' orders.

*God blesses those who patiently endure
testing and temptation. Afterward they will receive
the crown of life that God has promised to those
who love him.*

JAMES 1:12 NLT

———

Energy pulses through you, making your fingers drum and your feet twitch. You want to get up and move, but you're not allowed. Whether your restrictions are temporary or permanent, losing your independence can strip away your sense of humanity, not to mention your patience. If only you could do something other than watch the world go by.

My friend, even though your restrictions may push you past the point of sanity, you can ground yourself in God. He doesn't always promise an easy road, but He does promise to give what you need for each step of the journey. If you need more patience, He offers it. If you need a safe outlet for your energy, He'll point the way.

He can turn every drum of the fingers into a song of praise, every twitch of the feet into calm assurance. As you let Him reshape you, He will bless you with a new outlook—a vision that sees beyond these frustrations and looks ahead to the "crown of life."

It may not be easy to persevere, but God will provide what you need for this moment.

Will you seek your peace in Him?

—m—

Dear Lord,

It's hard to sit still when I just want to get up and move the way I used to. I know my restrictions are for my good, but it's hard to keep perspective when my independence has been stripped away. Relying on others is a test of patience, especially when they can't help me as quickly as I'd like. Sometimes it's tempting to take my frustration out on them, but I know it won't make me feel any better.

As I find myself stuck in this place, will You move me from restlessness and train my focus on You? I'm all too aware of my limitations, but I know You are a God with no limits. Your patience, love, and grace stretch beyond anything I can imagine. Will You give me a measure of each right now?

As I sit here reading, please settle me with Your presence. Show me what it means to live content in all circumstances, to avoid dwelling on *what isn't* and accepting *what is,* with faith and trust. Whenever I find myself waiting on others for help, I ask for Your grace to fill me. Enable me to see my caregivers through Your eyes and to be grateful for their help, rather than letting my frustration get the better of me.

I'm thankful that even when I struggle—when my restlessness spills out in harmful ways—Your love knows no limits. You continue to watch over me, providing what I need. The road may not be easy, but You promise to reward my perseverance as I take each step.

Father, I ask You to give me an eternal perspective, to see that You have more for me beyond the frustrations of today. When my body fails me, I place my trust in You and commit to pressing on even when it's hard.

In Jesus's name, amen.

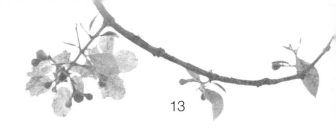

13

When You Feel Self-Conscious

For those who are embarrassed
about their appearance.

*When they arrived, Samuel took one look at Eliab and
thought, "Surely this is the LORD's anointed!" But the
LORD said to Samuel, "Don't judge by his appearance
or height, for I have rejected him. The LORD doesn't see
things the way you see them. People judge by outward
appearance, but the LORD looks at the heart."*

1 SAMUEL 16:6-7 NLT

———

One look in the mirror, and your self-confidence plummets. The image staring at you is a sad shadow of the person you once were. Your skin tone, your hair, your weight—nothing looks familiar anymore. This physical condition isn't only wreaking havoc on your insides, it has changed the shell you present to the world.

50

As you battle these self-conscious thoughts, I pray you'll find solace in the words of the Bible. The prophet Samuel was charged with handpicking the next king of Israel. He went down the line of brothers presented to him, each one ruddy and handsome. Impressed by their appearance, Samuel thought surely they were God's chosen, but he was wrong. Opening Samuel's eyes to look past the impressive height, hair, and face, God said, "See what I see. I don't look at their outer shells; I look at their hearts."

Dear friend, what a beautiful reminder from the God who made *you*. While you see your altered appearance and worry what others will think, the One who matters most is looking at your heart. He sees you as His precious creation and accepts you wholeheartedly.

He doesn't want you to base your worth on what you see in the mirror; He wants you to find your worth in *Him*.

Will you do that now?

—m—

Dear Lord,

I feel shallow praying this prayer, but the truth is that I'm struggling with my appearance. My condition has not only changed the chemistry of my body, but it's changed the way I look too. I can't stand seeing myself in the mirror, knowing that visitors and medical staff see me like this. I wish I could show them who I was before this condition, but it won't change who I am now.

Lord, even as I struggle with my self-image, I'm thankful for the reminder that You don't see me the way the world does. From the beginning of creation, You've hand-selected Your anointed ones based on factors unseen. When I face these hard moments, questioning my worth, would You remind me that my value is found in You alone?

Especially when visitors come to call, and their dressed-up facade stands in sharp contrast to my appearance, I want to accept their visit with gratitude and love. I don't want my self-consciousness to take away from the fellowship we might share. Instead, I want to be at peace with who I am in You so I can bless others in return.

As backward as it seems, I believe You can use my appearance to accomplish more through me than if I looked perfect. I find comfort in the fact that King David was almost overlooked, fading in the shadow of his brothers, yet You handpicked him as Your chosen one. Could You do that for me? Could You take my brokenness and somehow use it for good?

I want to see myself through Your eyes in order to

catch a bigger vision beyond what the mirror tells me. As I draw near to You, I trust that You will replace my self-consciousness with self-love, and I commit to letting You use me however You choose.

In Jesus's name, amen.

14

When You Feel Trapped

For those who feel physically trapped in their hospital rooms or at home.

But God led His own people forward like sheep and guided them in the wilderness like [a good shepherd with] a flock. He led them safely, so that they did not fear; but the sea engulfed their enemies.

PSALM 78:52-53 AMP

———〰———

Whether you're at the hospital, a care center, or at home, the walls surrounding you may feel like a prison. Day in and day out, you stare at your surroundings and wonder if you'll ever leave. Maybe instead of a building or a room, your *body* feels like the prison, trapping you inside your condition with no hope of escape.

Wherever you find yourself, I pray you'll draw comfort from the constant presence of God. The Israelites

54

pent forty years in the desert—forty long years trudg-
ng through sand and heat! And yet God walked with
:hem, providing daily manna to sustain them for the long
ourney.

You may be facing your own wilderness, slogging
:hrough one painful moment at a time, but you can rest
n God's plan. Just like He offered the Israelites a cloud
:o lead them by day and a pillar of fire by night, He will
guide you one step at a time through your situation. He
promises to provide what you need.

Will you keep your eyes on Him?

Dear Lord,

I'll confess I'm tired of being stuck in this place day
in and day out. As I stare at the same walls and my body
fights the same struggles, I wonder if I'll ever escape. I
find myself tempted to grumble and complain, to focus
on my problems and let discontentment consume me,
but I know that will only make me more miserable.

Can You draw me away from noticing only the negative? Even if my physical surroundings don't change,
I want a shift in perspective so I can see You at work. I
trust that You're providing what I need each day, just as

You led the Israelites through the wilderness, so I ask for courage to follow where You lead.

I'm grateful for this place of shelter You've provided even when it gets wearisome, and I ask You to help me notice the blessings here rather than the burdens. I know that being here is a necessary part of my journey, but if a change in scenery is needed to improve my healing, would You make that clear? If it means getting outside for a few minutes or taking a short walk down the hallway, show me how I can renew my spirit through simple movements.

If You're keeping me here to grow something within me, give me the vision to see it and the willingness to change. If You're asking me to reach out to someone here, don't let me miss the opportunity. As I learn to view these surroundings as a blessing, help me to share Your peace and love with those I meet.

I'm thankful for Your care, and I commit to seeking Your hand in all things.

In Jesus's name, amen.

15

When You Feel Weak

For those whose bodies are
sapped of strength.

*Have mercy on me, L*ORD*, for I am faint; heal me, L*ORD*,
for my bones are in agony.*

PSALM 6:2

*He gives strength to the weary and
increases the power of the weak.*

ISAIAH 40:29

———

Everyone runs out of strength from time to time,
but when it happens to you, it can turn your world
upside down. Simple tasks you used to do with ease sud-
denly require more energy. Your muscles feel like foreign
objects inside your skin. Will you ever feel like your normal, healthy self again?

Whether you're recovering from surgery, dealing with an injury, or facing a long-term disability, physical weakness can drain the strength from your body *and* your spirit. Frustration, discouragement, and exhaustion are its by-products.

Just as the psalmist poured out his heart, you can offer your unfiltered prayers to God right now. Even though your physical body may fail you on this earth, God is all-powerful. He will meet you in your weakness and fill you with His strength. It may not take the form of bulked-up muscles, but it will mean a soul at peace—a mind and heart that know your true strength comes from within. He invites you to call out to Him and lean on His mighty name.

Will you let Him fill you up now?

—m—

Dear Lord,

I'm so frustrated by the lack of strength in my body. I try to do basic tasks that used to be easy, and I can't get my muscles to do their job. I'll admit it's exhausting, but most of all, it's taking a toll on my mind and heart. My emotions are on edge because of the physical struggle.

I lose patience with myself and my caregivers, and the last thing I want is to put a wedge in my relationships. Is there any way this weakness can be taken from me?

Whether it's Your will to remove my weakness or not, please fill me with the physical strength I need to get through today. Whatever my next task, I ask You to help my body meet the challenge. If it's part of my healing to experience discomfort—to push myself a little past my comfort zone to get stronger—give me the willpower to press on. I recognize my body is working overtime to respond to my condition, so I ask for patience as it does its job.

Thank You for the amazing way You've designed my body to function and heal itself. If my weakness is a sign that I need to slow down, help me to accept that. Calm my mind so I can get the rest I need.

No matter how my body responds, I want to seek my strength in You. I praise You for being all-powerful and full of might. Sometimes I fall into the trap of believing my recovery is based on my strength alone. I know that will only lead to disappointment. Will You remind me of the help You provide? When I'm tempted to give up or complain, fill me with a fresh renewing of energy in my spirit.

I'm grateful that You can use my weakness as a canvas for Your strength. I ask for vision to see my condition as a way to bring glory to You, and I commit to staying grounded in Your power.

In Jesus's name, amen.

16

When You Get Bad News

For those who receive a bad prognosis.

Don't panic. I'm with you. There's no need to fear for I'm
your God. I'll give you strength. I'll help you.
I'll hold you steady, keep a firm grip on you.

ISAIAH 41:10 MSG

When anxiety was great within me,
your consolation brought me joy.

PSALM 94:19

———— ∿ ————

The moment you've feared has arrived. You've received a phone call or seen the somber look in your doctor's eyes, and you know life will never be the same again. While you've dreaded this moment all along, you now find yourself walking through a new door that leads to more questions and fear.

What are the next steps? Will I make it through?

While the trials of life threaten to pull you under, God invites you to come to Him. He promises to meet you in this place of anxiety, to hold on to you with His firm grip. Your mind may swirl with the impact of your news, but He can ground you with His love.

As you grasp His hand, He'll soothe the panic bubbling inside. He longs to guide you each step of the way, keeping you steady for the path ahead.

Will you cling to Him now?

—⁓—

Dear Lord,

I'm reeling from the news I just received. At times I feel panic rising up inside me, making it hard to think and breathe. Other times I feel numb, paralyzed by the weight of it all. I can't help but think about what this means for my future—not just my future healing, but the days and weeks ahead of me. I feel trapped inside this prognosis with no way out.

Not only do I fear what's ahead, I also feel let down by my body. Even though I know this life is temporary, it's still sobering to realize my body is fragile and susceptible to failure. I never imagined this would be my journey, and yet here I am.

As I face the days ahead, please remind me that You never fail. My life will never be the same again, but You remain unchanged, steady, and present through each step I take. When anxiety overwhelms me, cover me with Your peace. Steady my breathing and my mind, as I rest in You.

Even though I don't know what the outcome will be, I trust that You do. In my moments of doubt, draw me to Your Word so I can be reminded that Your plan is always sovereign. You've never failed Your people, and You won't start now.

When fear threatens to cloud my vision, lift my eyes above the worries of this prognosis. Show me what it looks like to walk in trust. Give me the courage to seek You for my strength, even when it's not easy.

I know I can't get through these next days and weeks on my own, so I look to You for my comfort and help.

In Jesus's name, amen.

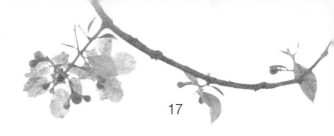

17

When You Have to Make a Hard Choice

For those making a decision with
weighty consequences.

*Though the Lord gave you adversity for food and suffering
for drink, he will still be with you to teach you. You will
see your teacher with your own eyes. Your own ears will
hear him. Right behind you a voice will say, "This is the
way you should go," whether to the right or to the left.*

ISAIAH 30:20-21 NLT

———〜〜———

When decisions are staring you down, the medical implications can be daunting. Whether it's choosing a treatment plan or deciding whether to have surgery or not, you feel the weight of the possible outcomes bearing down on your shoulders. What if you make the wrong choice? What if there's another way you're not seeing? What if the consequences impact not only you, but those you love?

As you battle the questions and confusion, I pray you'll seek your answers in God. He is the ever-present Teacher, walking with you and offering His guidance. It may not be an audible voice, but it may be a prompting to ask another question, or an experience of a friend that points the way.

Confusion and fear will try to crowd in, drowning out your ability to hear God's will. Even when the right choice isn't apparent, you can turn to Him for wisdom, trusting He'll make the right path clear in His perfect timing.

Will you lean into Him now?

———— ᨀ ————

Dear Lord,

I'll admit I feel inadequate to make the choice ahead of me. When I think about the possible outcomes—whether it's physical pain, more time in doctors' offices, or continued strain on my emotions and relationships—I become overwhelmed. I wish I wasn't in this position to begin with, having to make such a weighty decision, but the reality is I'm here. I need Your help to know what to do next.

As confusion sets in, please ground me in the guidance only You can provide. I know You may not reveal the right path with an audible voice, but I ask for clarity of mind to think through the options, without worry clouding my judgment. When fears creep in, help me release them to You so I can know and understand Your will.

Thank You for being the Great Teacher and Guide along this journey. I'm humbled that You love me enough to be invested in each aspect of my care. I know You've placed doctors and advisers along my path to help me through this decision. If I need to seek guidance beyond my current caregivers, help me to recognize that. Enable me to listen to their words and weigh the pros and cons, but even as I take them into consideration, remind me to seek Your wisdom above all others.

Give me unmistakable peace. Rein me in if I'm tempted to jump to a decision too quickly. As the answer becomes clear, I pray for courage to follow the right path, even if it's scary or not what I originally hoped for.

I commit to walking with You through each step of this process, and I thank You in advance for the guidance You'll provide.

In Jesus's name, amen.

18

When You Miss Home

For those who miss the comforts
of the familiar.

*Those who live in the shelter of the Most High will find
rest in the shadow of the Almighty. This I declare about
the Lord: He alone is my refuge, my place of safety; he is
my God, and I trust him.*

PSALM 91:1-2 NLT

———⁓———

A soft bed, a home-cooked meal, familiar sights and
smells—all of these taunt you with their absence.
Instead, your world is filled with unappetizing food,
beeping monitors, and constant interruptions. Sometimes you just want a taste of *home*.

Whether you're at the hospital, a care facility, or other
temporary lodging, rest in the fact that you're not alone
in your struggle. Your environment may be draining your

strength, disrupting your sleep, and fraying your emotions, but God has walked this entire road with you. He's with you even now.

Psalm 91 says He provides shelter and a place of safety. His type of shelter isn't built with bricks and wood. It's girded with peace and protection. You may long for your physical home, but what if you found a home in God's presence? What if you drew near to Him wherever you are and rested in the shadow of His wings?

Your physical surroundings may not change, but He promises to comfort your soul. He alone can turn your longings into a deeper trust and rest.

Will you come to Him now?

—⁓—

Dear Lord,

I confess I'm tired of being in this environment filled with unfamiliar sights and sounds. As I'm faced with yet another interruption or unappetizing plate of food, I find it hard to be patient with my circumstances. Will I ever feel the comforts of home again?

Thank You for the reminder that even though this place is foreign to me, You provide a safe shelter. Forgive me when I lose sight of Your love and care. I sometimes get caught up in my struggle and forget that You're here with me now. I know You're not limited to a particular place and time—even this one where I find myself.

Although this setting doesn't feel as warm and homey as I'd like, I'm thankful You've provided it as a place to find healing. Help me remember that sometimes discomfort is necessary to get better, and fill me with patience when I'm craving home.

If it's possible, could You bring comforting reminders to get me through this time? Whether small or big, I want to appreciate the gifts You provide every day. Open my eyes to the blessings around me, even if my surroundings don't change. I want to carry a spirit of gratitude and peace, rather than grumbling and complaining about my problems.

Bring me back to You when I slip into a habit of discontentment, and ground me in Your Word so I'm filled with Your peace. Thank You for offering a place of refuge and shelter. As I struggle to feel at home in this environment, I come to You and rest in the safety You provide.

In Jesus's name, amen.

19

When You Need a Second Opinion

For those who need guidance beyond their doctor's expertise.

The foolishness of God is wiser than human wisdom, and the weakness of God is stronger than human strength.

1 CORINTHIANS 1:25

While you wish you could always trust your doctor's advice, you may have times when you feel uneasy about an answer you're given, or you wonder if someone with more experience would view your situation differently. Your condition is unsettling on its own, but adding an unclear direction rocks the boat even more.

Where should you look for the right answer? And

more importantly, how will you *know* when the right answer comes?

As you navigate this murky sea of opinions and expertise, you can find assurance in the God whose wisdom knows no limits. The Bible says His foolishness exceeds the wisdom of the most knowledgeable person on earth. Your doctors have valuable input, but their words are trumped by the One who sees all and knows all.

While you're trying to discern whether to follow your doctor's plan or seek another opinion, you can draw from the guidance God provides. He won't lead you astray. As you listen to Him, He'll fill you with clarity to see the next step in front of you.

Will you let Him lead you now?

—⁂—

Dear Lord,

I feel uneasy about my doctor's plan, and I'll admit it's unsettling. Part of me wants to just move forward so I don't have to start over with someone else, but I also don't want to go down the wrong path. So much is at stake with my care. I can't afford to move forward without thinking through all the possibilities, so will You calm my mind so I can think clearly?

When impatience presses in, help me remember that You promise to provide enough light for the next step I need to take. My search for answers may continue, but You see the whole picture. As I seek guidance for the next step now, please open my eyes to where You want me to go. Show me which doctors can provide the best answers for my situation. Guide me to the right resources and people who can recommend the type of care I need. It's overwhelming to begin the search for another physician, but I don't want to leave any options unvisited.

Help me to keep coming to You for guidance, no matter where I am on this path. As I visit other doctors and get their advice, I ask for clarity to know which one is the right caregiver for me. I know Your wisdom far exceeds that of any human, but I also know You've prepared certain doctors with the knowledge and experience my condition needs.

Guide me to the one You have in mind, and show me how to continue walking in trust, no matter where You lead.

In Jesus's name, amen.

20

When You See No Way Out

For those who've lost their vision beyond
the current circumstances.

*Then Moses stretched out his hand over the sea,
and all that night the LORD drove the sea back
with a strong east wind and turned it into dry
land. The waters were divided, and the Israelites
went through the sea on dry ground, with a wall of
water on their right and on their left.*

EXODUS 14:21-22

*Wait for and confidently expect the LORD; be strong
and let your heart take courage; yes, wait for and
confidently expect the LORD.*

PSALM 27:14 AMP

—⚬—

All you see in front of you is the struggle you fight
every single day. Your former pain-free life is a

distant memory, and hope for a future life has dimmed until it's become a black hole. You're stuck in this condition and see no way out.

If this describes you, I pray you're comforted by the story of Moses leading the Israelites across the Red Sea. After God delivered them from Egyptian slavery, His people soon found themselves hemmed in on every side. The Red Sea stretched in front of them, and the Egyptian army closed in behind. As horses' hooves pounded nearer, shaking the earth, God parted the waters and provided a way through.

Dear friend, you may be emotionally and spiritually spent right now, seeing no way out of the situation bearing down on you. You might see only problems and insurmountable odds, but you can rest in the fact that God is moving ahead of you. His work may not be visible through miraculous signs and wonders, but it can be felt in the changing of a heart, the lifting of a spirit.

As you put your hope in Him, He'll help you see beyond the present moment. He longs to fill you with strength and courage for whatever this day may bring.

Will you let Him?

—⁓—

Dear Lord,

I've become so buried in my situation that I'm

struggling to see how this road will ever end. I feel boxed in, with nothing but dark walls surrounding me. Is there any hope for joy to fill my life again? It feels so phony to act happy when I'm stuck in this place of hardship and pain. I don't ever want to put up a false front. At the same time, I know I'll be miserable if I stay here.

Lord, if there's any glimmer of hope, would You reveal it to me? Please show me how these walls could be colored with light. I know You are the all-powerful God who can provide escape through great seas, and I ask You to provide a way out for me if it's in Your will.

Even if You don't change my physical circumstances, I ask You to change my heart. Open my eyes to see those around me who need Your love. I know I'm not the only one hurting. If there's any way I can come alongside others and share in their struggles, give me courage to do so.

I pray for Your peace to fill me as I walk this road. Thank You for seeing the future and working in this situation, even when I don't see all the pieces coming together. Like the psalmist, I want to wait for and confidently expect what You will do through me. Give me patience to wait on Your timing, however long or short it might be, and help me to trust You in all things.

In Jesus's name, amen.

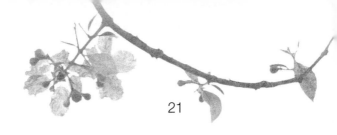

21

When You Want a Moment to Yourself

For those who need a break from visitors.

In the day of trouble he will keep me safe in his dwelling; he will hide me in the shelter of his sacred tent and set me high upon a rock.

PSALM 27:5

———

D o you ever find yourself craving a moment of quiet? While some minutes are filled with loneliness, others are filled with unending medical exams, doctor check-ins, or back-to-back visits from well-wishers. Maybe you're sharing a hospital room with another patient, so the interruptions are doubled.

If time to yourself feels like a far-off dream, let the psalmist's words bring rest to your soul. As noise and conversation fill your head until it's about to explode, God can quiet you with His love. He set the example through His Son, who intentionally withdrew from others to pray. As Jesus spent time with His Father, hiding in the shelter of His dwelling, He was refilled for the tasks in front of Him.

Perhaps you can take steps to reduce the interruptions in your life. But if not, remember your heavenly Father offers a safe dwelling place, inviting you to find solace in His arms alone. He can draw you away from the noise of this world to find peace.

Will you let Him do that now?

—ᴍ—

Dear Lord,

I feel bad for growing weary of the interruptions in my life. I know well-wishers want to cheer me up, and doctors and nurses are simply doing their job to help me heal, but sometimes I need a minute to myself. The noise never seems to stop. Just when I think I'll have some peace and quiet, another visitor comes.

When I sense my frustration building, will You remind me that You are the only source of rest and peace? I'm thankful for the people You've placed in my life, and I want to live with gratitude, not impatience, so I ask You to fill me with grace even when I need time to myself.

If I need to set boundaries around my time, show me how and when to do so. I recognize I'll never be refilled unless I spend time alone with You. If these interruptions are causing an emptiness in my soul, reveal that to me and enable me to make the changes necessary to connect with You again.

Whether I'm able to change my circumstances or not, please continue to draw me to Your side. I'm so thankful for the safe shelter You offer. I don't want to miss it. I recognize that this is a constant need, so bring me back to You whenever I sense the disconnect in my spirit.

I want to catch a glimpse of Your eternal purpose. If there's any way I can share Your love with those in my company, give me the vision to see their needs. I commit to coming to You alone as my source of rest, and I ask You to flood my soul with Your supernatural peace.

In Jesus's name, amen.

22

When Your Closest Relationships Suffer

For those whose condition
has placed a wedge between
them and their loved ones.

*This is what the LORD says: "When I bring Israel
home again from captivity and restore their
fortunes, Jerusalem will be rebuilt on its ruins,
and the palace reconstructed as before.
There will be joy and songs of thanksgiving,
and I will multiply my people, not diminish
them; I will honor them, not despise them."*

JEREMIAH 30:18-19 NLT

———◦———

You don't want the rift to happen, but it cuts a gap in your closest relationships anyway. While you struggle with your physical condition, your connection to your loved ones suffers the fallout. Less time together and less common ground, more stress and misunderstandings—all of these take their toll. Perhaps you're left with the feeling that you don't know your loved ones at all anymore.

Dear friend, if you've felt this divide, draw comfort from the reminder that God can restore anything that's been broken. Even if your relationships are in ruins, with nothing but rubble to show for them, you can bring the pieces to God with an earnest heart. Hurtful words, abandonment, lack of understanding—He can take each one and build something new and beautiful.

Even if you have no influence over your loved ones' actions, you can find refuge in God. He promises to love you unconditionally, to provide a home for you. As you seek His help, He'll show you how to respond to your loved ones with forgiveness and understanding.

Will you allow Him to help you now?

—∿—

Dear Lord,

I'm hurting over the divide that's growing between my loved ones and me. This condition has challenged so many aspects of my life, and it seems the physical struggle has only added to the tension in my closest relationships. I know my situation has created new burdens for my loved ones, putting more pressure on their time, money, and emotions. I wish it didn't place this wedge between us, but it feels like we've become strangers trying to navigate the same trial on completely separate roads.

Lord, forgive me if I have placed any unrealistic expectations on them. I know my condition has demanded more of them than I can imagine. If I've added to their burden unnecessarily, please make that clear to me. I want to right any wrongs and take steps toward reconciliation, rather than widen the gap between us.

If my loved ones have committed hurtful actions toward me, please fill me with forgiveness. I know it doesn't always come easy, but with Your help, I want to release them to You rather than holding on to bitterness and pain.

Above all, I'm thankful for the reminder that You can rebuild our relationships. As I see these broken pieces of rubble around me, I offer them to You. I ask You to carry each one and build a new wall. Not a wall that divides, but a wall that unites and protects.

Show me what the first step needs to be. Whether

my loved ones meet me in the middle or not, I want to live in the peace You provide. Help me to rest in Your grace, and to extend that grace to my loved ones as we navigate this difficult time.

In Jesus's name, amen.

When Your Faith Is Gone

For those who've lost their hope in God.

We are pressed on every side by troubles, but we are not crushed. We are perplexed, but not driven to despair. We are hunted down, but never abandoned by God. We get knocked down, but we are not destroyed.

2 CORINTHIANS 4:8-9 NLT

———⁓———

If you were to collect your faith in a jar, it would be empty. Or maybe a few small drops would plop into the bottom, but not enough to sustain you for an hour, let alone days or weeks. As your condition presses in, pushing you through one disappointment after another, you may find yourself questioning how God could possibly care…or maybe whether He exists at all.

Dear friend, I know He may seem far off and uninterested, but I plead with you to keep seeking. Let Paul's

words in the Bible remind you that even when life per-
plexes you, hurts you, and knocks you down, God will *not*
let you be destroyed.

If anyone knew what it felt like to be pressed on every
side, it was the apostle Paul—a man who faced shipwreck,
imprisonment, and brutal persecution. Just when God
provided a victory or a way out, Paul took another blow.
And yet he never took his eyes off the One who gave him
unwavering hope.

You may feel emptied of your faith and struggling to
see any sign of light, but even in the fiercest trials, God
promises He'll never abandon you.

Will you follow Paul's example and find your hope
in Him?

—⟨⟨⟩⟩—

Dear Lord,

I'll confess my faith is gone right now. I wish I could
say I'm trusting in You through this situation, but that
would be a lie. My condition has led to so much disappointment and pain that it's hard to imagine You could
possibly care. I find myself questioning why You would
let me go through this, not to mention whether You
have a plan for my healing.

As I face these doubts and questions, I acknowledge

that my spirit feels dry. This lack of faith has drained my emotions, and the edges of my soul are cracking from the emptiness inside. Is it possible You can fill these cracks and give me life again? The Bible says You're the Living Water. If that's true, I want Your hope to flood my soul. Even if it starts as a small trickle, I want the kind of water that won't run dry each time I face a hardship, but sustains me through this trial and test.

Thank You for the example of Paul. I'm encouraged that others have faced hardships before me and still found hope in You. I want to be filled with that kind of vision—to see beyond my doubts and trust that You're here with me now.

There's no easy way out of my situation, but perhaps there's purpose in the struggle. As I test out these wobbly legs of faith, remind me that You don't always promise to spare me pain, but You do promise to pull me out of the pit of despair. Whether my physical condition changes or not, I want to draw comfort from Your presence.

Guide me to Your Word when the doubts creep in, so Your truth can silence the lies that choke my trust. I'm grateful You remain by my side, even when I doubt. I ask You to fill me with the faith I need to get through this day.

In Jesus's name, amen.

24

When Your Life Feels Out of Control

For those who feel like the
reins have been tugged
from their hands.

I am leaving you with a gift—peace of mind and heart.
And the peace I give is a gift the world cannot give.
So don't be troubled or afraid.

JOHN 14:27 NLT

I have told you these things, so that in me you may have
peace. In this world you will have trouble.
But take heart! I have overcome the world.

JOHN 16:33

Your hands long to grasp something solid and firm, to be able to control what happens next. Yet here you are, being carried along with no say, no ability to pull your spinning world to a stop. Whether it's circumstances that have swept over you or doctors' orders that dictate your next move, you may be reeling from the fear that you'll never have control of your life again.

If you're fighting this unease, I pray you'll draw comfort from the peace Jesus offers. He says it's a gift you won't find anywhere else in the world. It's found only in Him. Can you imagine a life of peace right now? It may seem impossible or far away, but what if it was as close as a prayer?

God understands the struggle you face. He knows the world brings trouble and fear. But He doesn't leave you to face your trial alone. When life feels out of control and you're stuck on a course you feel powerless to change, lean into God's sovereignty. He may let you walk on rocky paths at times, but He is always in control and can be trusted in all things.

Will you look to Him now?

—◈—

Dear Lord,

I hate this feeling of having no control over my

circumstances. Sometimes I feel as if I'm suspended in the air by a giant crane, dangling while I wait for someone else to determine my fate. It's unsettling to be in this position, to know I have no say in what comes next.

Even though it's hard to relinquish control, I'm thankful for the medical team working on my behalf. I know You've given them the training and tools to treat my condition, and I want to trust them to do their job well. When I'm tempted to let discouragement sink in, settle me in a place of peace and show me how to put my faith in You alone.

I know You're sovereign over all things. When I'm grasping for something solid to hold on to, please draw me to Your side. Show me truth in Your Word so I can remember You always have a plan and are working for my good.

If my need for control is rooted in pride, please reveal that to me. It's not easy to admit I don't have it all together, but I know it's the first step to being more like You. As I face the reality that I can't control this situation, I want to allow You to shape my response. Show me what a humble spirit looks like, so You can receive the glory.

Above all, thank You for being the true source of

peace in a world riddled with fear and trouble. As I dangle in this unsettling place, I look to You to ground me. I believe You're ultimately in control, and I commit to releasing the unknown to Your care.

In Jesus's name, amen.

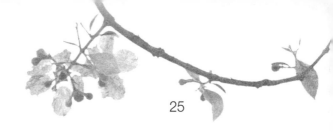

25

When You're Admitted to the Hospital

For those receiving focused medical care.

No one is abandoned by the Lord forever. Though he brings grief, he also shows compassion because of the greatness of his unfailing love.

LAMENTATIONS 3:31-32 NLT

—⁓—

Whether you've been admitted to the hospital for a specific period of time or indefinitely, your world may feel tipped on its axis right now. Maybe you're relieved to be here so you can receive the medical care you need. Maybe you're discouraged by what feels like a backward step. Maybe you're scared of what lies ahead.

No matter where you find yourself, remember God

hasn't abandoned you. He sometimes allows you to walk a different path than you expected or moves you to a new environment, but His love is unfailing. He was with you before you were admitted to the hospital. He's here with you now.

While you may be discouraged or worried about this next step in your care, draw from the presence of the One whose peace can't be matched. His compassion exceeds anything you can imagine, even in this uncertain place. He will help you through.

Will you place your hope in Him?

———~m~———

Dear Lord,

I have mixed emotions as I settle into my hospital room. In some ways, I'm thankful for the focused medical attention I'm receiving so I can get well again. But at the same time, discouragement and fear are bubbling under the surface. I'm disappointed that my body has failed me and sent me to this place.

I wish I could snap my fingers and make the situation better, but I know that's not possible. All I can do is trust in Your plan, even when it's hard or doesn't make sense. I'm thankful for the reminder that You haven't abandoned me. Please flood me with Your presence as I walk through these next hours and days.

I also ask You to be with those who are charged with my care. I know You've hand-selected the doctors and nurses who will be treating my condition, and I ask You to give them wisdom as they navigate the next steps of treatment. Guide their decisions, and fill them with clarity if there's any confusion or if test results are unclear.

As I wait for healing, I ask You to transform my doubts and fears into unwavering trust. I'm so thankful for Your love and compassion, and I'm humbled You care enough to be here with me now. Even when I can't see the path ahead, I place my worries in Your hands and commit to finding my hope in You.

In Jesus's name, amen.

26

When You're Bored

For those who wish they had something
to pass the time.

*I pray that God, the source of hope, will fill you
completely with joy and peace because you trust in
him. Then you will overflow with confident hope
through the power of the Holy Spirit.*

ROMANS 15:13 NLT

*Therefore encourage and comfort one
another and build up one another,
just as you are doing.*

1 THESSALONIANS 5:11 AMP

—∾∾∾—

Your fingers drum as you stare at the wall. Out of all
the challenges you've faced in your condition, you
never expected boredom. Yet here you sit with nothing

to do. Maybe you're stuck in a bed or chair with orders to limit your movement. Maybe you're waiting in a doctor's office, and the minutes are ticking by at molasses speed.

Whatever the cause, this is a perfect opportunity to turn your mind to God's goodness. Yes, you may be facing challenges, but there are blessings to be found too. How has God helped you during this time? Whom has He placed in your life to bring joy and hope? Maybe this place of boredom can be used to journal your gratitude or to encourage someone else through a smile or caring words.

Even in this finger-drumming state, your heavenly Father can fill you with purpose. As you remember the help and comfort He's provided, allow Him to open your eyes to those who might be blessed through your testimony. He longs to share His love through you.

Will you let Him?

—⁓—

Dear Lord,

I'll admit I'm tired of sitting around with nothing to do. Sometimes it feels as if my healing churns at a painfully slow pace. The hurry-up-and-wait game is exhausting as I long for something to happen. During these empty hours, I find myself focusing on my boredom, which only makes the time tick slower.

Would You shift my focus off my situation and onto Your blessings? Thank You for the reminder that there are gifts to be found, even in the trials of life. While I look for ways to pass the time, fill me with reminders of how You've provided in the past. I'm thankful You offer purpose and joy in all circumstances. In this time that feels purposeless, I ask for a flood of praise to fill me.

If there's anything I can do to encourage someone else, please bring them to mind right now. Open my eyes to see those around me, whether they're in this room or not, and show me how to lift their spirits. Whether it's creating something, writing a note, or offering a smile, I want to be a vessel for Your love.

You've been such a faithful provider, meeting my needs and walking with me on this journey. I don't ever want to forget Your goodness, even when my circumstances try to crowd You out. I commit to keeping my eyes on You, and I'm thankful for this opportunity to pass Your blessings along.

In Jesus's name, amen.

27

When You're Caught by Surprise

For those facing an emergency they
didn't see coming.

God is our refuge and strength, an ever-present help
in trouble. Therefore we will not fear, though the earth
give way and the mountains fall into the heart of
the sea, though its waters roar and foam and the
mountains quake with their surging.

PSALM 46:1-3

———

hen emergencies happen, the world seems to
throw you into a tailspin, shaking the core of
your life until you're paralyzed by fear. So many worries to wrap your brain around: What's wrong with your
body? Will you make it through? What other pieces of

your life need to be squared away in response to this crisis?

Whether your emergency lands you in the hospital or you're coping with it at home, I pray you'll draw comfort from this passage in Psalms. You may feel the force of the waves battering you with worry and fear, but even in the swirl and surge, God is a Solid Rock.

If fear is choking your trust, bring it to your Savior. Allow Him to meet you in the vortex and provide strength and peace in the waiting. It may seem impossible to find peace when your world is uprooted, but help can be found in Almighty God, who never wavers.

Will you seek refuge in Him right now?

—⁓—

Dear Lord,

I'll confess I'm fighting against fear of what lies ahead. Everything has happened so fast. It's hard to wrap my brain around the implications for my health, not to mention all the other pieces of life that are scrambling to catch up.

As I navigate this storm, will You calm my mind? Fear can spin frightening scenarios, and I don't want to let them paralyze me. Help me to focus on the step in front of me, instead of looking too far into the future. I know You'll provide what I need for this moment, but it's hard to settle into this pocket of time and be at peace.

My mind is also spinning with the responsibilities left hanging while I deal with this crisis. Work, home, and family are put on hold. I can barely cope with the situation in front of me, let alone tie up all the loose ends elsewhere. As I struggle to keep up, please provide the help I need to make the appropriate contacts with my loved ones.

Thank You for the reminder that when my life is turned upside down, You remain a Solid Rock. I feel the pressure of the waves crashing over me right now, but You stand firm. Draw me to Your side whenever I feel weak. Protect me. Fill me with Your strength. I want to be at peace in the midst of the unknown, so I place my trust in You, regardless of what comes next.

In Jesus's name, amen.

28

When You're Confused by Medical Jargon

For those who don't understand the medical explanations given to them.

If you need wisdom, ask our generous God,
and he will give it to you.
He will not rebuke you for asking.

JAMES 1:5 NLT

The LORD gives wisdom; from his mouth come
knowledge and understanding.

PROVERBS 2:6

—⁓—

Medical staff talk to you, but they might as well be speaking a foreign language. Whether they're explaining your condition or giving instructions for the next steps of your care, their words go into your ears like a secret message you can't decode. You know they're talking about your body, but the disconnect to your brain leaves you helpless and frustrated.

If you're struggling to decipher the explanations given to you, I pray you'll draw comfort from God's guidance and wisdom. You may be confused right now, perhaps struggling with feelings of inferiority, but God isn't perplexed or overwhelmed. He's the Great Physician, who knows what's going on inside of you. He understands every medical term because He created the words that are spoken and the people who say them.

As you navigate these confusing words, draw near to the One whose wisdom exceeds anything known to humanity. Ask Him for knowledge and understanding, for clarity and discernment. He promises to provide what you need in abundance.

Will you turn to Him now?

—✺—

Dear Lord,

I hate not being able to comprehend the words spoken to me, especially when they have such a direct impact on my body. As medical staff talk to me, I find myself feeling frustrated and "less than" because I can't understand terms that are second nature to them. What if I miss something important, and the results send me backward in my care?

Lord, as I fight the confusion and worries, please settle my mind so I can think clearly. I don't want my frustration to grow until it clouds any chance of understanding. Clear the fog from my mind so I can catch the most important information.

If I need to ask questions for clarity, give me wisdom to know what to ask and how. Bring people to my side who can help decipher the explanations given to me. Your Word says, "Though one may be overpowered, two can defend themselves. A cord of three strands is not quickly broken" (Ecclesiastes 4:12). Would You help me see those near me who can weave a cord of discernment on my behalf?

I'm so thankful for the doctors and medical staff You've charged with my care. Even though I don't always understand their words, it's comforting to know You've given them the knowledge they need to treat my condition. When I battle inferiority, remind me that You've handcrafted each of us as individuals, giving us the exact gifts and talents we need. Help me to be grateful for my unique design, rather than letting comparison knock me down.

Above all, thank You for being the Father of wisdom. I believe You are the all-powerful, all-knowing God. I look to You for discernment as I navigate each step of my care.

In Jesus's name, amen.

29

When You're Embarrassed or Humiliated

For those who've been poked
and prodded to the point
of embarrassment.

*He takes no pleasure in the strength of a horse
or in human might. No, the LORD's delight is in those
who fear him, those who put their hope
in his unfailing love.*

PSALM 147:10-11 NLT

*He raises the poor from the dust and lifts the needy
from the ash heap; he seats them with princes and has
them inherit a throne of honor.*

1 SAMUEL 2:8

—⟋⟍—

Doctors and nurses perform their duties with thousands of patients, so to them it's a job. But to you it's personal. From the moment you put on a hospital gown, you feel vulnerable. What comes after donning the hospital gown can leave you downright embarrassed. Maybe your humiliation doesn't involve a paper-thin gown, but you're still forced to endure a test or procedure that reveals body parts usually kept hidden.

Whatever your situation, rest assured God's love for you isn't based on what others see or do. It's based on the fact that you're His unique creation—designed for a purpose only you can fulfill. When you're in an awkward situation or humbled to the point of discomfort, remember that He delights solely in your heart for Him.

You may feel knocked down or even violated as your body is poked and prodded, but God promises to raise you up from this moment, to lift you up with dignity and honor. He sees you as His precious child and will never abandon you.

Will you turn to Him now?

Dear Lord,

It's so hard to be in this vulnerable position. Sometimes when I'm poked and prodded, I feel like part of an assembly line rather than a human being with feelings and emotions. The reality is, my condition forces me to reveal parts of my body I'd prefer to keep hidden. Even though I know it's necessary for healing, and my medical team is just doing their job, it leaves me feeling embarrassed and downright humiliated at times.

As I battle this self-consciousness, will You draw my eyes away from my situation and focus my heart on You? It's hard to stay strong during these tests and procedures, but I know You can ground me in Your love. I don't want to merely survive the embarrassing moments; I want to get through them with grace and dignity.

Give me patience to allow the medical staff to do their job. I know they have my healing in mind, so remind me of that when I'm tempted to forget. Thank You for the blessing of modern medicine and the knowledge that's guiding my care. When I get lost in my own world of embarrassment, help me remember that my procedures and tests are not only necessary but also a gift.

I don't always see how You could use these moments to raise me up to a place of honor, but I'm thankful for the reminder that You delight in my heart. As I come to You for my comfort and strength, give me a humble spirit to accept these circumstances with peace and trust. No matter how I feel, I want to shine Your light and spread Your love.

In Jesus's name, amen.

30

When You're Facing Death

For those who will soon leave this world.

Even though I walk through the darkest valley,
I will fear no evil, for you are with me;
your rod and your staff, they comfort me.

Psalm 23:4

I heard a loud voice from the throne saying,
"Look! God's dwelling place is now among the people,
and he will dwell with them. They will be his people,
and God himself will be with them and be their God.
He will wipe every tear from their eyes. There will be
no more death or mourning or crying or pain, for the
old order of things has passed away."

Revelation 21:3-4

Your life has been lived, and now you face your final days. Whether you've been told these are your last hours on this earth, have received a dire diagnosis, or you're heading into a life-threatening procedure, a flood of doubts and fears may wash over you.

Maybe you've accepted Christ as your Savior, but still you question. Is everything you've been told about salvation true? Will your loved ones be okay once you're gone?

Maybe your foundation of faith is rocky at best, and you fear what's ahead. Is there really a heaven? Will you ever see your loved ones again?

As you grapple with what will be on the other side, I pray these Scripture verses remind you that your Shepherd is walking beside you, and His words are true. If you've turned to Him in faith, He has a place waiting for you in heaven. If you haven't turned to Him, it's not too late. He longs to welcome you into His forever home—a place where crying and pain will be no more.

Will you rest in Him now?

—⁓—

Dear Lord,

It's hard to wrap my mind around the fact that these may be my final moments on earth. As I think about what's on the other side, I'm struck by the fleeting nature of life. All my accomplishments, work, and relationships are pared down until I'm left with this failing body and memories of those I love.

I won't deny I'm fighting doubts and fears right now. What will be on the other side of death? I don't know the answer, but I'm thankful You do. Thank You for sending Your Son, Jesus, to die on the cross for my sins. I acknowledge that He purchased my way to heaven. I accept Him as my Lord and Savior. As I face these final days, remind me that my confession of faith is secure in You. Your words are true, and You've prepared a place for me in heaven.

I look forward to being in Your presence, to experiencing no more crying or pain. Before that day comes, I ask that my pain on this earth would be minimal. If I need to seek help from medical staff to make these final days as calm as possible, give me the strength and courage to ask.

Lord, my heart is especially heavy for those I love. As I think about their lives beyond my death, I worry about how they'll cope with the loss. Give me physical strength to say the words I need to say to them, whether it means expressing my love, righting wrongs, or seeking forgiveness. I don't want any lingering bitterness or pain to be left in my wake, so help me find the right ways to communicate anything that's been left unsaid. Cover my loved ones with Your presence after I'm gone so they're strengthened for the road ahead.

Above all, thank You for walking through this valley with me. I draw near to You for comfort in these moments and place my soul in Your hands.

In Jesus's name, amen.

31

When You're Lonely

For those who are yearning for company.

*I am with you and will watch over you wherever you go,
and I will bring you back to this land. I will not leave
you until I have done what I have promised you.*

GENESIS 28:15

———

An empty room is your only companion, and the seconds tick painfully by. Family, friends, and caregivers have already visited or finished their tasks for the day. Now it's just you with your thoughts. You may have activities to occupy your hands and mind—a book to read, TV show to watch, or crossword puzzle to solve—but what you really want is someone to talk to.

Dear friend, in these quiet moments, don't forget your heavenly Father is here with you right now. He's walked this road with you all along and promises to remain wherever you go. Picture Him pulling up a chair next to you, His mouth curving in a welcoming smile, an unspoken invitation for you to bask in His presence.

As you unload your burdens and fears, He'll cover you with His peace. He promises to watch over you, to stay by your side. While loneliness gapes like a cavern in your soul, He longs to fill you with His love. Only He can satisfy your deepest longings for connection.

Will you reach out to Him now?

—⚬⚬⚬—

Dear Lord,

As I battle loneliness, I'll admit that it's hard to stay positive and upbeat. My condition already leaves me feeling isolated, but this quiet room seems to amplify the emptiness inside of me. Being alone with my thoughts can be a dangerous thing. I try to fill my time with activities, but I still fall into worry or discouragement.

Please cover me with Your peace right now. I often find myself turning to temporary distractions, thinking they'll fill the void, but deep down I want someone to talk to who will understand my struggle. While people can encourage me along the way, I know You're the only One who will satisfy my deeper need for companionship.

When I forget this, please bring me back to You. Draw me to Your Word so I can be filled with truth. Give me a strong yearning to connect with You in prayer so I can better understand Your heart.

I'm so thankful You never leave me, and You watch over me always. As You fill my emptiness, I ask for eyes to see new friendships You might provide. Maybe this time can be used to push me out of my comfort zone as I reach out to someone else who's hurting. Don't let me miss them while I sit here by myself.

Whether other people are in my room or not, I don't want to fill my time with activities that will leave me feeling emptier. I want my need for connection to be satisfied in You alone. I trust that You're here with me now. I commit to resting in Your presence no matter what my circumstances are.

In Jesus's name, amen.

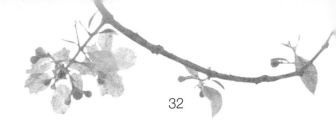

32

When You're Needed Somewhere Else

For those who can't fulfill responsibilities
at work or home.

*You can be sure that God will take care of everything
you need, his generosity exceeding even yours in the
glory that pours from Jesus.*

<small>PHILIPPIANS 4:19 MSG</small>

W hile you sit here fighting your condition, your
mind ticks through the list of responsibilities
you should be doing instead. Work, home, family, vol-
unteering—they weigh you down with the reminder
that you're not there to fulfill them. Your helplessness
boils over into frustration and worry. How will others
cope in your absence? Will they carry extra burdens to
fill your void?

As you fight the heaviness pressing in on you, remember that you may not be able to meet all the needs of your loved ones, but God can. He is the Great Provider—the One whose generosity extends beyond anything you can imagine. Not only is He providing for you in your current situation, He is with those who feel your absence. His presence isn't limited to this room you occupy. He is everywhere.

While you're unable to fulfill responsibilities elsewhere, rest assured God is moving. He knows what is needed in the places you can't be. He'll fill any gaps created by your condition.

Will you put your trust in Him?

—∽—

Dear Lord,

I feel so helpless sitting here, knowing other people need me and I can't be there for them. Sometimes I see the burden in their tired faces and stooped posture. Other times I imagine their struggle even though I can't see it firsthand. It's hard enough to cope with my condition, let alone the guilt of letting down my loved ones.

Lord, as I battle this frustration, I'm thankful You are everywhere at all times. I feel as if I'm trying to hold on to my life with a tight grip, but it's slipping between my fingers. Help me loosen my hands and acknowledge that I can't be all things to all people. Only You can. I don't understand why I'm battling this condition, but the reality is I can't change it. Show me how to accept these circumstances and trust that You can fill in the gaps elsewhere.

If pride is at the core of my frustration, please reveal that to me. It's hard to admit I'm limited in what I can do, but I want the humble faith to trust in You. When worry creeps in, settle me with the reminder that You're with my loved ones. I may not see the extent of their struggle, but You do.

I ask You to make Your presence real to them right now. Whatever tasks they're trying to fill in my absence, give them what they need. If I can help from afar, reveal those opportunities to me. Even if it's continuing to pray or expressing my gratitude, show me how I can ease their burden. I want to use this time to thank and encourage rather than wallow in self-pity or guilt.

Thank You for providing what's needed in all places, at all times. I'm grateful for Your presence and ask for Your strength to shine through my weakness.

In Jesus's name, amen.

33

When You're in Pain

For those who are physically hurting.

*Our momentary, light distress [this passing trouble] is
producing for us an eternal weight of glory [a fullness]
beyond all measure [surpassing all comparisons, a
transcendent splendor and an endless blessedness]! So we
look not at the things which are seen, but at the things
which are unseen; for the things which are visible are
temporal [just brief and fleeting],
but the things which are invisible are
everlasting and imperishable.*

2 Corinthians 4:17-18 amp

———〰———

Pain rips through your body, making it hard to con-
centrate on anything else. While it wreaks havoc on
you physically, it can also drain your emotions and spirit.
You may find yourself frustrated with your circumstances,

your caregivers, or even with God. Why won't He take the pain away? Can't He see you're suffering down here?

Dear friend, when your pain seems endless, I pray you'll find hope in the reminder that it won't last forever. Jesus felt excruciating pain on this earth too. No medicine was available to ease the sting of the nails in His hands or the crown of thorns on His head. He not only understands your struggle, He offers His presence to get you through.

What a blessing and comfort! You may see no purpose in your pain, or you may wish it could be erased completely, but keep holding on. Even when your physical struggle seems unbearable, God can draw you close and give you His peace.

Will you let Him do that now?

———— ✦ ————

Dear Lord,

It's hard to keep a clear head when this pain is pulsing through my body. Sometimes it's so bad that I lose hope that it will ever get better. I find myself losing patience with myself and with my caregivers. I'm not proud of the times my frustration has spilled over. I wish there was a better solution to manage my pain, but even if there isn't, I want to be able to get through it with patience and trust.

Thank You for the reminder that the pain of this earth is fleeting. Even though it feels like it will last forever, You promise to give me peace that transcends my physical struggle. I want that peace right now, Lord. Whether the sting of my physical pain is eased or not, I want to see beyond this moment and sense Your presence.

If I can take steps to reduce my pain, would You reveal them to me? If medication isn't the right answer, give me grace and peace to accept that. I want to be content no matter what my circumstances are, so help me view this situation through Your eternal lens.

I believe You're here with me now. I'm so thankful You know the depth of my pain because of the sacrifice Your Son made on the cross. Help me keep my heart trained on You so I can keep this situation in perspective. When a new wave of pain comes over me, flood my mind with reminders of who You are—my Helper and Provider, my Sword and Shield, a faithful God who walks me through the fiercest storms.

Thank You for Your promises. As I train my thoughts heavenward, I commit to seeking my help solely in You, and I trust that You'll flood me with Your peace.

In Jesus's name, amen.

34

When You're Physically Tired

For those whose bodies are exhausted.

Even youths will become weak and tired, and young men will fall in exhaustion. But those who trust in the LORD will find new strength. They will soar high on wings like eagles. They will run and not grow weary. They will walk and not faint.

ISAIAH 40:30-31 NLT

—〜〜—

E xhaustion presses in on you, weighting your eyelids with the pull of sleep. Whether you're tired because of medication, lack of rest, or the effort your body requires to heal, you feel powerless to do anything but lie in bed. Maybe you find yourself giving in to your body's demands, or maybe you're fighting against them.

Whatever the case, let your soul find comfort in the words of Isaiah 40. You're not alone in your battle with exhaustion. Even the strongest men and women become weak and tired. But what a beautiful reminder that true strength isn't based on physical performance; it's based on where you place your trust.

When your body drags with the weight of fatigue, you can turn your eyes to the One who never grows weary. He provides the strength you need for this moment, no matter your energy levels. Allow your body to get the rest it craves, but more importantly, allow your soul to find peace in God's shelter. He promises to renew your spirit for the day ahead.

Will you let Him?

— ∿ —

Dear Lord,

I'm so tired of feeling as if I can't do anything but sleep. Not only is my body drained, but my mind and emotions feel emptied too. My head is constantly in a fog. I can't summon the energy to interact with others the way I wish I could. Is there any end in sight? I just want to feel like a normal human being again.

Thank You for the reminder that I'm not the only one on this earth to deal with exhaustion. Even the strongest of us feel tired and weak at times. It may not fix my current situation, but it's comforting to know I'm not the only one who struggles.

While I find myself wishing for more physical strength, I know that the most important area to nurture is my spirit. It's hard to imagine being energized anywhere right now, but I trust You can give me what I need. If my exhaustion is a result of medication or choices that can be reversed, give me wisdom to see that. At the same time, if sleep is a necessary part of my healing, help me to be at peace rather than fighting against it.

Lord, more than anything, I'm thankful Your strength is greater than any power I can imagine. I know Your glory is displayed most effectively through my weakness, so remind me of this when I get discouraged or frustrated.

Focus my eyes on You at all times. Whether You allow me to walk without fainting or soar as high as the eagle, I trust that You'll renew my strength for the demands of today.

In Jesus's name, amen.

When You're Preparing for Surgery

For those who will soon go into
the operating room.

The LORD himself goes before you and will be with you;
he will never leave you nor forsake you.
Do not be afraid; do not be discouraged.

DEUTERONOMY 31:8

———w———

Sometimes surgery is a last resort. Other times it's a gateway to hope. Many times it's a combination of the two.

While you're preparing to put yourself in the doctors' hands, a multitude of worries may crowd in. Will the pain be unbearable? Will your body handle the changes it undergoes? Will the procedure resolve your medical concerns, or will it leave you with more questions?

Whatever worries are swirling through your mind, remember that God not only walks beside you, He's one step ahead of you too. He's here with you right now, and He's also in the operating room with the surgical team as they prepare for your procedure.

In these tense moments, He offers you His courage and strength to face the next steps, whatever they might bring. The all-powerful, all-seeing God is walking *with* you and *before* you. What an honor and blessing!

The other side may be unknown to you, but it's known to Him.

Will you rest in His care?

—⁓—

Dear Lord,

As I face these moments before surgery, I'm feeling nervous. I'm trying to get my mind off what is about to happen, but fear keeps crowding in. The unknown is a scary place to be. Giving myself over to anesthesia and the surgeons' hands feels anything but safe, but I know it's what I need to get better.

Thank You for the reminder that You are with me in this moment. As I battle my nerves, will you cover me with a sense of Your presence? Fill me with peace that can come only from You. Strengthen me to face this next step with courage and trust.

Even though surgery is nerve wracking, I'm thankful for the medical staff who have been trained to treat me. I bring them to You now, Lord. I pray You will fill the operating room with calm assurance as they prepare for my surgery, and carry that sense of calm into the minutes that follow.

As I move into the operating room, I pray for all aspects of the procedure to be under Your mighty hand. May each one of the surgeons' tools function properly and serve their intended purpose. May the amount and type of anesthesia be appropriate for my body, and may any adverse reactions be minimized when I wake up.

Lord, please guide and direct each person involved in my care. Give the doctors vision to see any trouble spots while they operate. Steady their hands to do the work before them efficiently and accurately. Surround them with medical staff who work together as a team, supporting each other for a successful outcome.

Most of all, I pray that, regardless of the surgery's results, I will remember that You are my ultimate Caregiver. Humans can care for my physical needs, but only You can soothe the worries flooding my soul. I turn to You now and give these next moments to You.

In Jesus's name, amen.

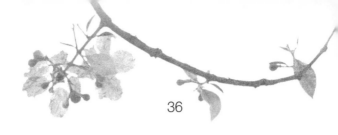

36

When You're Ready to Give Up

For those who've lost the will to fight.

I say to God my Rock, "Why have you forgotten me? Why must I go about mourning, oppressed by the enemy?" My bones suffer mortal agony as my foes taunt me, saying to me all day long, "Where is your God?" Why, my soul, are you downcast? Why so disturbed within me? Put your hope in God, for I will yet praise him, my Savior and my God.

PSALM 42:9-11

———~~~———

If only my pain would end... Has your mind uttered these words? If so, my heart aches for you because I too have lived in that place of darkness—the place that tells us there's no reason to fight. Whether your suffering is emotional, physical, or both, you might be thinking of ways to escape the agony, maybe even thinking it would be easier to take your own life.

Dear friend, don't let the lies of the enemy snuff out your hope. There *is* a reason to live. You may feel alone in your struggle, your condition squeezing the joy out of you, but God created you with His own hands and finds you worthy of living.

No one can duplicate your place on this earth. Whether your condition keeps you here for one more week or one more decade, there is purpose in these days you're given.

While you face this moment of despair, remember that God welcomes you in your brokenness, just as you are. He doesn't require a false happy front to be His child. As you bring your pain to Him, pouring it out at His feet, He can plant a seed of hope within you, giving you strength to fight for one more day.

Will you come to Him right now?

—m—

Dear Lord,

It's hard to put into words how exhausted I am from fighting my condition. There are moments when I feel drawn toward the easy out—to escape this pain forever—but somehow I keep hanging on. I don't know how much longer I can do this. Loved ones try to stay upbeat. They're not always willing or able to handle the dark thoughts I struggle with, but I'm glad You can handle them. I bring them to You now and openly acknowledge that I'm struggling.

Is it possible for You to turn these shadows into a seed of hope? If so, I want that, Lord. I want a seed of hope to be planted so I can find a reason to fight again. I want my life to have a purpose outside of this pain, so will You show me what that could look like?

Thank You for creating me with Your own hands. Forgive me for not viewing my body as You do. I've viewed it as disposable and unworthy, instead of seeing it for what it truly is—a creation of the Most High God. I proclaim in Jesus's name that You have made me worthy in Your sight. Through Your Son's death on the cross, my life has value and purpose.

Even if I struggle to see that purpose right now, I commit to seeking it. I trust You'll fill me with the desire to live in Your will, to see outside my struggle and look for ways You can use me. Joy feels far away, Lord, but I know You can restore it within me again.

I place my life in Your hands and seek my strength in You alone.

In Jesus's name, amen.

37

When You're Scared
of the Unknown

For those who are battling fear.

*Now, this is what the LORD says—he who created
you, Jacob, he who formed you, Israel: "Do not
fear, for I have redeemed you; I have summoned
you by name; you are mine. When you pass
through the waters, I will be with you; and when
you pass through the rivers, they will not sweep
over you. When you walk through the fire, you will
not be burned; the flames will not set you ablaze.
For I am the LORD your God,
the Holy One of Israel, your Savior."*

ISAIAH 43:1-3

———〰———

Fear can stretch its tentacles into your life without
warning. You may be at peace one moment, and the
next your mind is playing out every possible scenario

until you're suffocating from anxiety. Whether it's fear of pain, a diagnosis, or the worries of tomorrow, you may struggle to see anything beyond the panic.

My friend, let this passage of Scripture remind you that you don't have to see the future to be at peace. God created you. He formed you with His own hands. He's not going to leave His precious creation to face this journey alone. Even if you find yourself walking through a rushing river or a blazing fire, He won't let you bear more than you can handle.

As fear crowds in, take a deep breath and make space for God's presence. Let Him loosen the tension in your muscles and fill your mind with peace. He has called you by name. He has bought you with a high price. He's walking this road with you, holding your hand through it all.

Will you let Him carry you now?

———— ᴍ ————

Dear Lord,

I'll admit I've let fear crowd in. Sometimes it suffocates me, making it hard to breathe and think beyond the moment. Scenarios play out like a movie reel, and each one steals a little more oxygen from my lungs. I hate this feeling, and yet I'm powerless to change it.

Lord, I'm thankful that in the midst of my fear, You've never left my side. In my tense moments, I tend to forget You created me and have a plan for my life. At times it feels like a cruel path You've made me walk. I feel the rush of the river sweeping over my head—the burn of the fire as it licks my wounds. Yet You are the Living Water—a water that refreshes and cools.

I beg You to fill me with that water now. Where fear is suffocating my peace, revive me with Your comfort. Where worries are blinding my sight, help me see the vision You have for me. I trust that You have a plan, even in the midst of my pain. I loosen my grip on these circumstances and release them to Your hands.

In the moments when I struggle, turn my eyes to You. Remind me of Your goodness, Your love, and Your presence walking beside me each step of the way. I believe the words in the Bible are true, so I choose to trust You even when life doesn't make sense.

The future might be unclear to me, but You see it all. Help me to rest in Your sovereign plan and place my fears at Your feet.

In Jesus's name, amen.

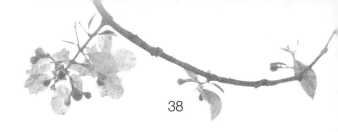

38

When You're Tempted to Ignore Instructions

For those who are tired of following doctors' orders.

Then [Jesus] returned to the disciples and found them asleep. He said to Peter, "Couldn't you watch with me even one hour? Keep watch and pray, so that you will not give in to temptation. For the spirit is willing, but the body is weak!"

MATTHEW 26:40-41 NLT

—~~~—

Following your doctors' orders can be downright exhausting, whether it means resting an injury when you want to move, taking medication that tastes horrible, or staying home when you're stir-crazy. Even though you know the instructions are for your good, it's hard to be patient when you're craving freedom.

If you find yourself struggling to follow doctors' orders, I pray you'll find comfort in the fact that Jesus's own followers fought against their bodies' natural bent. In the final days before His death, Jesus asked His closest friends to keep watch while He prayed nearby. As He poured His anguish out before His Father, His disciples fought yawns, their eyelids growing heavy until they gave in to the tug of sleep.

My friend, while it may be tempting to give in to what feels most comfortable right now, remember you can always strengthen your willpower in the presence of God. He calls you to keep watch and pray, to turn your struggles over to Him and allow Him to shape your response. Whatever orders you're tempted to ignore, draw near to Him and ask for alertness and strength.

Will you do that now?

——ww——

Dear Lord,

I'm struggling to stay the course right now. Even though I know my doctors' orders are necessary for my healing, it's hard to stay patient. I find myself thinking it wouldn't hurt to ignore a little instruction here or there, but I know those thoughts are based on my frustration, not grounded in truth.

I don't want to do anything that would delay my healing, so please keep my eyes focused on You. I know I'm not able to stand strong on my own, but You can fill me with willpower to do what's right. When temptation crowds in, remind me of the reasons for medical instructions. Help me face the reality of my condition and take the necessary steps in front of me.

If any restrictions could be eased, help me frame the right questions to my doctors. If their answer isn't what I hope for, give me the grace to accept my situation and walk with strength.

I recognize that the ultimate root of my temptation is pride—whether it's wanting to be seen as capable and knowledgeable, or wanting to be seen without this condition clouding people's judgment. If there's any pride driving my decisions right now, I ask You to reveal it to me and give me the courage to address it. I know You can use these restrictions to heal my body and bring glory and honor to Your name.

Thank You for the medical care I'm receiving. I trust that You've equipped my doctors with the knowledge to plan the next treatment steps for me. I commit to taking care of my body wisely. Strengthen me to do what's right, even when it's hard, so Your name alone will be praised.

In Jesus's name, amen.

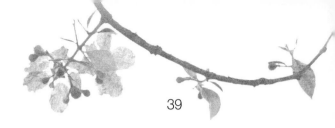

39

When You're Tired of Taking Medication

For those who don't want to take another pill.

A cheerful heart is good medicine,
but a broken spirit saps a person's strength.

PROVERBS 17:22 NLT

Medicine feels like a necessary evil sometimes. It eases the symptoms of your condition, but it also introduces new burdens. Some medications taste nasty, while others are big and awkward going down your throat. And some bring on horrible side effects. Maybe you have a medicine bottle filled with pills that do all of this and more.

If you're weary of taking medication of any kind, I pray this verse in Proverbs encourages you. While medicine improves the condition of your body, the best remedy for your soul is a grateful heart. This isn't a phony, fake cheerfulness, but a heart tuned to God, ready to offer praise in all circumstances.

Your physical condition may not change, but you can choose your outlook. A positive spirit gives life to your soul, while a negative spirit saps your strength. What a sharp contrast God offers. As you battle the realities of your situation every day, imagine what would happen if you viewed life differently—if you acknowledged the hard but didn't let it steal from the good.

You may not be able to stop taking pills, but God longs to give you peace in the process. He can take your mind off your medical routine and give you joy.

Will you allow Him to do that now?

—⁓—

Dear Lord,

I'm so tired of taking pill after pill. They're not fun to swallow, and I wish they didn't come with side effects. Even though I know they were prescribed in my best interest, I'm sometimes tempted to skip them altogether. I know that's not the right choice, but it seems that I'll never feel normal again.

Even though I'm weary of medication, I'm thankful it eases the symptoms of my condition. Keep me on track when I want to quit. Thank You for the doctors who have prescribed these remedies for me. I ask You to fill them with wisdom as they continue to monitor my progress. If I can be released from any medications, please point the way and give me guidance to know when and how to ask. I want to be wise in taking medicine that's helpful, but I also don't want to put anything in my body that isn't needed.

Whether my medical routine changes or not, I'm thankful for the reminder that You've given me the ability to choose my outlook. I ask for gratitude to fill my soul right now. When I'm tempted to complain, remind me of all the ways You've worked in my situation. Give me eyes to see the beauty in life's difficult moments.

I recognize that a positive spirit can soothe my heart like no physical cure can, so I bring my frustrations and burdens to You. Lift them from my shoulders, and fill me with an outlook that transcends my circumstances. I praise You for being such a caring God. I commit to coming to You as my only source of joy.

In Jesus's name, amen.

40

When You're Transitioning from Hospital to Home

For those who have been discharged
from the hospital.

Forget the former things; do not dwell on the past.
See, I am doing a new thing!
Now it springs up; do you not perceive it?
I am making a way in the wilderness
and streams in the wasteland.

ISAIAH 43:18-19

———ᵡᵡᵡ———

Mixed emotions flood you. Finally you got the answer you've wanted to hear: You're going home. With this news comes excitement, but it can also bring new worries. While the comforts of home are a blessing, you may wonder how you'll cope without focused medical attention. Maybe you've been sent home with pages of instructions, and you're hoping you don't mess anything up.

Wherever you are right now, let this be an opportunity to express gratitude to God. As your anticipation rises, take this time to recall all the ways He's been faithful. Whether you've experienced healing or it's still off in the distance, let your heart fill with praise. Give Him the glory and honor for making a way in the wilderness.

If worry is crouching under the surface, allow Him to replace it with trust. He understands the journey you've traveled, and His steady hand will remain with you in this next step. He longs to steady you with His presence and joy.

Will you let Him?

—— ∾ ——

Dear Lord,

As I make this transition back home, I have mixed emotions. I'm so thankful to leave the hospital environment, especially the interruptions, noises, and uncomfortable beds, but I also know there's still healing to be done. My days in the hospital brought many ups and downs. I know coming home won't magically take those things away, but I'm grateful to return to the comforts I missed.

As I navigate the joys and challenges ahead, I want

my heart to stay tuned with praise. No matter how hard the past days have been, I'm grateful You're doing a new thing. My healing may not be complete, but You've allowed me this gift of coming home.

I know these next days won't necessarily be easy. There are still concerns to watch for, and I worry about missing something important. Even though I'm glad to leave the hospital, I feel uneasy not having access to quick medical aid. As I monitor my progress at home, please make me aware of any symptoms that require a call to my doctor. I don't want to overreact if it's not important. At the same time, I want the wisdom to realize when I need help.

Show me how to navigate my relationships with those at home too. Our lives have been uprooted by my hospitalization, and I know we'll have an adjustment period getting back to our new normal. Fill me with grace and love for them, especially those who are assisting with my care. I ask You to give them strength and wisdom as we continue to follow doctors' orders.

More than anything, keep reminders of Your love and provision in front of me at all times. I'm thankful You've made a way in this wilderness, and I continue to trust in You.

In Jesus's name, amen.

41

When You're Waiting for Answers

For those who are anticipating test
results from the doctor.

*You made all the delicate, inner parts of my body
and knit me together in my mother's womb.
Thank you for making me so wonderfully complex!
Your workmanship is marvelous—how well I know it.
You watched me as I was being formed in utter
seclusion, as I was woven together in the dark of the
womb. You saw me before I was born. Every day of my
life was recorded in your book. Every moment was laid
out before a single day had passed.*

PSALM 139:13-16 NLT

—◦◦◦—

Whether you're in the hospital or at home, waiting
for answers can be agonizing. As the minutes
tick by, you may find your worries growing, stacking up
in a pile of fear and what-ifs:

What if the answer isn't what I hoped for?
What if the doctor can't see enough to make a decision?
What if I'm sent down an unbearable road?

In the midst of the what-ifs, let this passage in Psalms soften the edges of your fear. The intricacies of your body aren't hidden from God. With a love and precision only He could manage, He knit each part of you together. Every cell, nerve, and muscle was fashioned and formed by the God of the universe.

Your future may be unknown, resting on the examination of doctors as they study your condition, but God knows the answers. Whatever may come, He sees each part of you and is moving ahead of your results, preparing you in advance.

Will you rest in Him?

———ᗰ———

Dear Lord,

So many emotions are running through me right now as I wait for answers. When I think about the worst-case scenario, fear floods my mind. I worry about what it might mean not only for me, but for my loved ones. I feel paralyzed by the weight of it all. God, please keep my heart calm in the midst of these fears. Rein in my imagination when it gets out of hand, and settle me in a place of trust.

Another part of me is so weary from the waiting. I just want to find out what's wrong so I can move on with my life. While the minutes and hours tick by, fill me with patience to wait for Your timing.

Thank You for my doctors' commitment to providing the right answers. I pray You will give them wisdom as they analyze and study. Clear their vision so they can see what needs to be seen, and show them if there are any concerns. Bring to mind knowledge from their many years of training so they can be confident in their diagnosis. And help me remember that this time of waiting is necessary, that accurate answers can come only from thorough analysis.

Thank You for the reminder that You see what's going on inside of me even better than the doctors, and no matter what comes, You will lead me through. As I sit here waiting, remind me of this truth often. Turn my heart toward You so I can be filled with Your peace. Help me to focus on what I can do in this moment and leave the rest in Your capable hands.

In Jesus's name, amen.

42

When You're Worried About Finances

For those who don't know how
they'll pay their medical bills.

*The eyes of all look to you in hope; you give them their
food as they need it. When you open your hand, you
satisfy the hunger and thirst of every living thing.*

PSALM 145:15-16 NLT

———∿———

Each time you go through another procedure or doctor visit or receive another prescription, you can practically hear the money draining from your bank account. Bills are piling up, and each one adds more weight upon your shoulders. Maybe you're so weighted down that your knees are about to buckle.

Dear friend, I know your circumstances make it hard to trust God, but rest assured He will provide. It may not

145

come in the form of a giant paycheck, but rather in the shape of daily bread. He's your loving Creator—a God who doesn't leave you to deal with these burdens alone. He is aware of what you need right now and knows every cent in your bank account. He *will* make a way.

As you battle your worries, allow Him to ease the tension gripping you. Let His guidance lead you along this path, and trust that He'll give what you need for each moment. Only He can satisfy your needs and restore your hope.

Will you turn to Him now?

—⁓—

Dear Lord,

I'll admit my stress is piling up right now. As if my physical struggle weren't enough, these medical bills are about to drown me. The cost of my care is overwhelming, and when I look at the amounts due, I don't see how I can possibly pay them all. Each time I receive a new one, my anxiety climbs higher. Is there any way out of this mess?

When I read verses about Your provision, I find myself doubting sometimes. My brain sees basic math, and the result looks obvious. And yet I also find myself hoping there could be a way through this without being buried. I know Your ways don't always make sense compared to the ways of the world, so will You train my eyes on You alone?

When worry crowds in, settle me down. Help me recognize the ways You're providing my daily bread even now. I know worry and fear won't change anything that happens tomorrow. They will only steal my joy for today. Work a miracle in my heart and mind so I can see You moving.

If I can take any action to minimize my bills or generate extra income, please show me what to do. I know my condition limits me, but I don't want to miss any opportunities You might send. If it requires reaching out for help, fill me with humility and grace to accept that I can't do this on my own. Sometimes Your answers come in the form of other people, so give me the recognition to know if that's Your plan.

No matter what happens, I ask for an increase of faith during this time. I commit to doing what I can to ease this burden, but I place the ultimate result in Your hands.

In Jesus's name, amen.

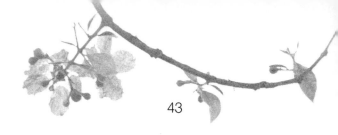

43

When You've Lost Patience

For those who want to be healed right now.

Every day I call to you, my God, but you do not answer.
Every night I lift my voice, but I find no relief. Yet you
are holy, enthroned on the praises of Israel. Our ancestors
trusted in you, and you rescued them.

PSALM 22:2-4 NLT

D o the psalmist's words echo the cry of your spirit
right now? Perhaps you've called out to God every
day and night—maybe weeks on end—but silence
greets you from the other side. While you know that trials produce perseverance, you scoff because you've had
plenty of opportunities for that. Now you just want to
be healed.

If impatience is fraying your nerves and curling your
hands into fists of frustration, turn to the God who invites

you to come to Him no matter how you feel. Patience seems to be required at every turn—waiting for doctors, fighting through the challenges of your condition—but God's grace begins where your limits end.

As you pour out your struggle, let Him cover you with His peace. You may not know when this journey will come to a close, but He does. He can take your impatience and fill you with trust.

Will you let Him do that now?

—⁓⁓—

Dear Lord,

My patience is completely spent. While I deal with my condition and the frustrating moments that come with it, I find myself wondering why You won't just heal me. It seems like a cruel plan to keep me in this situation when You have the power to change it. The psalmist's words definitely echo my own. Why aren't You answering or offering relief?

Even as I battle these questions, I want to be able to trust You. If there's any way I can turn my impatience into praise, please open my eyes to those opportunities. I may struggle to see how You're working now, but I can remember how You've provided for me in the past. I know that the same God who helped me before will do so again, so I ask for greater faith to believe that.

In moments when my patience is gone, please cover me with an extra measure of Your presence. I know You're the only One who can provide peace that passes all understanding, so I seek You for it now. Turn my attention from my problems so I can rest in You.

While I wish I could see the future and know Your plan for my healing, I acknowledge that You alone are sovereign. Fill me with a sense of purpose in these long, frustrating days, so I can shine Your light, rather than dwell in the darkness of doubt. I commit to placing my trust in Your plan no matter where You lead.

In Jesus's name, amen.

44

When You've Lost Your Identity

For those who don't know who
they are anymore.

God created man in His own image,
in the image and likeness of God He created him;
male and female He created them.

GENESIS 1:27 AMP

We are God's masterpiece. He has created us anew in
Christ Jesus, so we can do the good things
he planned for us long ago.

EPHESIANS 2:10 NLT

———

While your condition has changed you physically, you feel like a different person on the inside too. The activities that once defined you—work, church, and family—have turned into doctor visits, hospital tests, and hours spent in waiting rooms. The person you are now is a mere shell of who you once were. Will you ever feel like yourself again?

Dear friend, as you struggle to figure out who you are, I pray you'll draw encouragement from the reminder that your physical state hasn't removed your identity as a creation of God. When He created you, He made you in His image. He calls you His *masterpiece*.

Sometimes an artist has to leave confusion on the canvas for a time, but the result is always breathtaking. That's what the Master Artist is doing with you right now. This situation may feel anything but beautiful—and normalcy may feel like a lifetime ago—but God is continually adding new brushstrokes. He is renewing you and building depth into your identity.

Will you let Him?

———— ∞ ————

Dear Lord,

I find it hard to identify with the person I once was. The activities that used to occupy my time and attention seem to play out like a movie reel—distant, unfamiliar, and separate from the struggles I'm enduring now. I used to be so carefree, with no comprehension of the ways my life would turn upside down. I find myself yearning to go back to those days.

Even as I battle the challenges of my condition, I don't want to fall into self-pity. I acknowledge that in many ways I've lost my self-confidence and sense of purpose. So much has changed, and I don't think I'll ever view things the same again. But maybe that's the value of this experience—opening my eyes to see through a different lens.

Thank You for the reminder that You created me in Your image. I don't always feel like a masterpiece, but I love the idea that even famous paintings have to undergo different stages of "beauty." Give me grace to accept that this part of the journey is right where I'm supposed to be. As Your brushstrokes deepen my life, don't let me get stuck in disappointment. Help me look for ways You can use me where I am right now.

I may struggle to find pieces of my old self, but I know You're working in and through me. Fill me with patience in the difficult moments, and keep Your purposes and plans in my heart. I want my identity to be found in You alone.

In Jesus's name, amen.

About the Author

Sarah Forgrave is a wellness coach and fitness instructor who finds great joy in encouraging others toward their full potential in Christ. As someone who has spent considerable time in doctors' offices, Sarah knows the challenges and triumphs a health journey can bring. Her greatest passion is helping others connect the dots between body and spirit in her coaching sessions, fitness classes, and wellness seminars. Her writing credits include contributions to the webzine *Ungrind*, as well as several compilation books, including *The Gift of Friendship* and Guideposts' *A Cup of Christmas Cheer*. Outside of writing and teaching, Sarah is the busy mom of two young children and the wife of an entrepreneurial husband, who whisks her off on adventures all over the world. When she has a moment to herself, she loves to shop the aisles at Trader Joe's or curl up with a good book and a cup of tea.

Sarah blogs about health and faith at
www.sarahforgrave.com.

She can also be found on:
Pinterest: www.pinterest.com/SarahForgrave
Facebook: www.facebook.com/AuthorSarahForgrave
Twitter: @SarahForgrave

Acknowledgments

To Todd Hafer, Kim Moore, and the rest of the publishing team at Harvest House—you are truly an answer to prayer. Thank you for spreading hope with me.

To my agent, Mary Keeley—thank you for giving me wings to follow where God led, even when it was different than what we originally envisioned. I'm grateful to have you in my corner.

To my sister, Jenny, and my brother, Brian—it's hard to quantify all we've been through together. Even though we don't get to talk as often as we'd like, I count you among my best friends. Jenny, thank you for your invaluable input into the outline of this book. I hope I did it justice.

To my mom—your love and support have meant so much. Thank you for your feedback early on in the creation of this book. I know others will be touched because of your willingness to share.

To my dad—I still remember waking up with a bad dream as a child and having you read Philippians 4:8 to me. The Word continues to be my source of comfort, and I'm thankful to you for pointing the way.

To my husband and kids—you've loved me and stuck with me through a lot of ups and downs. I'm so glad I get to call you "home."

To my Uncle Wayne—your insights added meat to one chapter in particular. Thank you.

To Jen C.—I'll never forget your kindness during one of the darkest times of my life, and now I'm blessed to call you my mentor and friend. Your investment has left handprints all over these chapters.

To Sarah C., my Warrior Friend—your prayers and assistance got me through the windstorm of writing this book (and the whirlwind afterward). So grateful to have you standing in the gap for me.

To my writing friends near and far, especially Wendy Miller—you've made this solitary journey feel not so lonely. If I were to write all the ways you've touched my life, I'd have another book on my hands.

To learn more about Harvest House books and
to read sample chapters, visit our website:

www.harvesthousepublishers.com

HARVEST HOUSE PUBLISHERS
EUGENE, OREGON